and the betrayal you feel. Her ability to walk you dow[n] make your journey less scary and bolster your strengt[h] more trusted voice for reassuring faith and hope in your ~~relationship~~ [with your] husband would be hard to find.

DONNA VANLIERE, *New York Times* bestselling author and longtime friend

Bob and Dannah Gresh offer a key that can unlock men and marriages from the prison of sexual sin and shame. This is a struggle that a large percentage of men are dealing with worldwide, and yet there are precious few resources to guide us. The shame and fear of disappointing our wives is overwhelming and gives shame power. Dannah's writing isn't just for women. It gives men a glimpse into the real hurt and pain that this sin causes, but also provides a lifeline of hope that redemption is possible. **This book has the real possibility of becoming a timeless tool that will save marriages for decades to come.**

DARREN TYLER, pastor, Conduit Church

Every marriage experiences pain, disappointment, and the overall effects of brokenness. It is a school for learning to live out biblical love and forgiveness. With raw vulnerability and transparency, Dannah invites the reader into her own journey and helps women navigate through difficult seasons on their way to restoration. **A must-read that points to the grace, hope, and redemption we can only find in Christ.**

LAURA GONZALEZ DE CHAVEZ, director, Aviva Nuestros Corazones

Happily Even After is a true story. My husband and I have been friends with Bob and Dannah for twenty years. We've seen them walk through hard things. We've seen them trust God with impossible prayers. We've seen God faithfully restore their marriage. But that's not how I know this book is a true story. I **know it's a true story because, twenty years ago, Bob and Dannah shared this hope—these Bible verses, these tools, these insights—with us during our own marriage crisis. I know firsthand that God can hold two people together when the chasm appears too vast to breach. I know for myself that God can change hearts and minds and habits when they appear unchangeable. I know personally that sometimes, you just need to know there's hope. Let *Happily Even After* be a voice of hope for you.**

LAURA BOOZ, author, *Expect Something Beautiful: Finding God's Good Gifts in Motherhood*

I highly recommend *Happily Even After* because of its raw honesty and transparency coming from a place of real brokenness and yet healing. The story of Bob and Dannah Gresh is a testimony to the forgiveness of Christ that overcomes sin and brings restoration. The studies, references, and biblical foundation give hope that you too can find happiness even after the pain of betrayal and sexual sin. As a former pornography addict and sexual sinner myself, I can affirm the claims of this book that through Christ real repentance and change is possible.

LAURA PERRY SMALTS, author

This book has truly touched my heart and I feel incredibly blessed to have read it. For those of us who know this hurt, Dannah has carefully, thoughtfully, and lovingly articulated her and Bob's story, maintaining throughout that we strengthen ourselves in the Lord. It's written primarily for wives, however, you might have a daughter, sister, or friend and this may be their story—**I would encourage all women to read this book to expand their understanding and insight.** Thank you, Dannah and Bob, for faithfully surrendering your story to honor and glorify the Lord.

NICOLA SMITH, a reader from Scotland

I've been a pastor's wife since I was twenty years old. I have listened to and prayed for many women who chose to fight for their marriage despite their husband's immorality. **This is the book I would have shared with them if it had been in print!** In this book, Dannah and Bob have chosen to share their journey, and Dannah has created a path that feels like she is walking just ahead of women courageous enough to pursue healing for their hearts. I am asking the Lord to use this tool to redeem and restore many who need to hear the truth from someone who can say, "This is the way, walk ye in it!"

HOLLY ELLIFF, pastor's wife and women's ministry leader

Raw. Honest. Wise. Dannah speaks gospel help and hope to every heart wounded by betrayal trauma. Not only are these pages packed with solid advice, they portray a vision for covenant marriage that will inspire hurting women to walk the redemptive path with conviction and courage.

MARY A. KASSIAN, author, *The Right Kind of Strong*

Praise for *Happily Even After*

Few things hurt a wife more deeply than discovering that her husband has been sexually unfaithful. Pornography or any other extramarital sexual activity strikes at the heart of marital intimacy. **Dannah Gresh does not whitewash the pain. She does not offer an "easy fix," but she does offer hope.** She writes, not from an ivory tower, but as one who has experienced the pain and found redemption. If you are walking this road, you will find *Happily Even After* a welcome companion. I highly recommend this book to wives who are struggling and those who want to help them.

GARY D. CHAPMAN, PHD, author of *The 5 Love Languages*

You've picked up this book because you feel lost and hopeless. Friend, you are neither. The God of the universe is with you, inviting you to open your heart to His healing and wisdom. This book will not fix your broken marriage, but it will show you a path to spiritual maturity and life from a godly woman who has walked every step of this road. When Joseph confronted his brothers who had sold him into slavery, he said, "you meant evil against me, but God meant it for good, to bring it about that many people should be kept alive, as they are today." I can't help but think of this verse as I read through *Happily Even After*. Through the evil of betrayal and sexual sin, God has created a story of redemption to preserve the lives of many.

DR. JULI SLATTERY, bestselling author; cofounder, Authentic Intimacy

Dannah is no dry-land sailor. Her marriage has been pommeled at times with waves of disappointment, failure, and shame. But over the course of years, I have watched her and Bob find a lighthouse in the gospel, an anchor in the Scripture, a harbor in the covenant-keeping love of God. **Through their tears and fears, these dear friends of mine have found in Christ the mercy, grace, and hope to press on—together.** Out of the messiness and damage caused by the storms they have been through, God has created something of great beauty and enduring value. Happily Even After will show you how He can do the same in any life, any marriage, that will dare to cling to Him and take Him at His Word.

NANCY DEMOSS WOLGEMUTH, author; founder and Bible teacher of Revive Our Hearts

At last! A book that clears a pathway through the mess of exposed sexual secrets. In *Happily Even After*, noted author Dannah Gresh provides both the biblical truth and clinical evidence needed to win back the trust lost during the trauma of marital betrayal. This book is an invaluable resource, written from personal experience, for any who have lived through deception and disloyalty in their marriage, as well as for all those who long to offer hope to others hurting in this way. **Every pastor and counselor—indeed, every spouse—will benefit from Dannah's timely and tender book. Buy it. Keep it on hand. And use it to offer the miracle of redemption to those who feel abandoned and unlovable but who, through Christ, can once again hope to live happily—even after.**

JANI ORTLUND, Renewal Ministries

This is not your average marriage book. Equal parts honorable honesty and timeless Truth, *Happily Even After* will help you face the reality of your marriage—namely that you are a sinner married to a sinner—and an even greater reality, that Jesus is a God who redeems. Your marriage doesn't need the fairy tale. It needs the faith that God is willing and able to restore broken things.

ERIN DAVIS, author of *Fasting & Feasting* and longtime friend

One of our greatest fears as humans is the fear of exposure. *What will people do with me if they find out who I really am, what I've done, what I struggle with?* This fear is especially powerful when it involves the dark world of sexual sin. So **it is remarkable that the Greshes have written with such candor about their own struggles with sexual sin in their marriage. This book will provide great encouragement for those who have felt hopeless.** God still promises to redeem our life from destruction!

PETE KUIPER, LCSW, Crossroads Counseling of the Rockies

Pure truth . . . rigorous and radical honesty that leads to the ultimate healing of redemption! *Happily Even After* is ongoing and available. Take the journey!

MIKE BIVENS, MA Christian Counseling

I have known Bob and Dannah for over thirty-five years and can tell you that what you're about to read is true. I have watched them fight for their marriage like no other couple I know. You may think that no one understands what you are going through with your husband, but Dannah knows. Her experience, compassion, courage, wisdom, insight, and faith to believe that you can live *Happily Even After* are evident on every page. She understands the thoughts you're thinking

Happily
Even After

Let God Redeem
Your Marriage

DANNAH GRESH

FOREWORD BY BOB GRESH

MOODY PUBLISHERS

CHICAGO

All Scripture quotations, unless otherwise indicated, are taken from the ESV® Bible (The Holy Bible, English Standard Version®), Copyright © 2001 by Crossway, a publishing ministry of Good News Publishers. Used by permission. All rights reserved.

Scripture quotations marked NIV are taken from The Holy Bible, New International Version®, NIV®. Copyright ©1973, 1978, 1984, 2011 by Biblica, Inc. Used by permission. All rights reserved worldwide.

Scripture quotations marked NLT are taken from the *Holy Bible*, New Living Translation, copyright ©1996, 2004, 2015 by Tyndale House Foundation. Used by permission of Tyndale House Publishers, Carol Stream, Illinois 60188. All rights reserved.

Scripture quotations marked CSB have been taken from the Christian Standard Bible®, Copyright © 2017 by Holman Bible Publishers. Used by permission. Christian Standard Bible® and CSB® are federally registered trademarks of Holman Bible Publishers.

Scripture quotations marked BSB are taken from The Holy Bible, Berean Study Bible, BSB. Copyright ©2016, 2020 by Bible Hub. Used by Permission. All Rights Reserved Worldwide.

Scripture quotations marked NKJV are taken from the New King James Version®. Copyright © 1982 by Thomas Nelson. Used by permission. All rights reserved.

All emphasis in Scripture citations has been added by the author.

All personal stories in this book are used by permission.

Edited by Anne Christian Buchanan
Interior and cover design: Erik M. Peterson
Cover photo of pictures clipped to wire copyright © 2019 by martin-dm/iStock (1178573531).
Cover illustration of plant pattern copyright © 2019 by Asya_mix/iStock (1186132289).
All rights reserved for the images listed above.
Author photo: London Wolfe Photography, State College, PA
Cover family photos courtesy of Dannah Gresh

Library of Congress Cataloging-in-Publication Data

Names: Gresh, Dannah, 1967- author.
Title: Happily even after : let God redeem your marriage / Dannah Gresh.
Description: Chicago : Moody Publishers, 2022. | Includes bibliographical
  references. | Summary: "Jesus Christ can help you redeem the broken
  places of your marriage. Dannah helps you: stop pretending everything is
  okay, strengthen yourself in the Lord, fight for your husband instead of
  with him, discover 7 essential beliefs every marriage needs to survive
  broken places, participate in your husband's redemption story"--
  Provided by publisher.
Identifiers: LCCN 2022036859 (print) | LCCN 2022036860 (ebook) | ISBN
  9780802419828 (paperback) | ISBN 9780802498755 (ebk)
Subjects: LCSH: Marriage--Religious aspects--Christianity. | Love--Biblical
  teaching. | Forgiveness--Biblical teaching. | BISAC: RELIGION /
  Christian Living / Love & Marriage | RELIGION / Christian Living /
  Women's Interests
Classification: LCC BT706 .G745 2022 (print) | LCC BT706 (ebook) | DDC
  248.8/44--dc23/eng/20220928
LC record available at https://lccn.loc.gov/2022036859
LC ebook record available at https://lccn.loc.gov/2022036860

Originally delivered by fleets of horse-drawn wagons, the affordable paperbacks from D. L. Moody's publishing house resourced the church and served everyday people. Now, after more than 125 years of publishing and ministry, Moody Publishers' mission remains the same—even if our delivery systems have changed a bit. For more information on other books (and resources) created from a biblical perspective, go to www.moodypublishers.com or write to:

Moody Publishers
820 N. LaSalle Boulevard
Chicago, IL 60610

1 3 5 7 9 10 8 6 4 2

Printed in the United States of America

To Elizabeth "Tippy" Duncan

who has counseled my heart with Truth
for nearly three decades

a note to every reader

This book is for the woman who believes she is safe and hopes to rebuild trust and intimacy in her marriage after her husband has sinned. A key component of restoration is humble, authentic repentance and brokenness in your husband.

You are *not* safe in your relationship if you are experiencing sexual, physical, or verbal abuse or repeated trauma from flagrant sin for which your husband is not repentant. If that's you, put this book down and call someone who can help you get into a safe place.

contents

Bonus Content · Got Questions?

a note from bob gresh

Thirty-five years ago I met a girl named Dannah.

We fell in love, got engaged on stage in front of two thousand people, and had a fairy-tale wedding. And once we were finally man and wife, ~~we lived happily ever after.~~

~~we struggled a little, and then lived happily ever after.~~

we fought and laughed and cried and learned that happily ever after is a myth but discovered something even better: a love that endures every hardship.

Sometimes I wish my wife wrote about flowers or animals. She could write books on marketing or Middle East politics, and I'd be very happy. She writes about none of these. Instead, she pens thoughts about relationships and sex and truth and healing. And she doesn't write fiction—that's where the uneasiness sets in. Before you finish this book, you will know more about our marriage than I wish you to know, more about our failures and intimate moments than my pride wants to allow. Not that our marriage is unique. That's just it. It's not.

Dannah and I shared a glimpse of our story at a Revive Our Hearts conference in 2017. For twenty-three excruciating minutes, we invited a few thousand women to hear some of the private details of our pain and redemption. I wouldn't say we hung our dirty laundry in the front yard for everyone to see, but no one had to wonder what was still drying in the backyard.

After Dannah and I spoke that day, women lined up. For nearly three hours we prayed with wives who feared their marriages were over or that they were just going to have to live with the way things were. They wanted hope—needed to hear from someone that their marriages could be redeemed.

That day my heart was moved by what happened, and I knew this book needed to be written. I hope you'll be one of the women who will read it, identify with the heartache, and use the information to do the hard work of letting God redeem you . . . and your marriage, if your husband also puts himself in God's hands.

Some will not. The quest is both painful and risky. But if you choose to take it, you'll find the rich reality of the passion and intimacy you can only know after you've both failed and forgiven more times than you care to count. You'll begin to experience the kind of love that is possible when you both step in to participate in the redemption story God is writing in your lives.

I hope you'll choose to believe that you can be happy. Even after.

—Bob Gresh

how to use this book

One book won't fix a marriage.

And saving one takes two people who are willing to come together to discuss their problems.

But don't put this book down just yet if your husband is not willing to engage. I think I can help strengthen you to cope with the crisis you're facing alone, if necessary.

At the same time, please don't think of this as your end-all solution. It's meant to be a supplement to a more comprehensive plan. One reason we decided to share our story—and what we learned along the way—is there were too many treatment programs, books, and people that were presented as a one-stop fix-all solution.

That's ridiculous!

Your story is unique, and you'll need to discover God's redemption tools for your own heart and marriage. I encourage you to do whatever it takes to experience full healing as an individual and, if possible, as a couple.

To help you in this work, my husband, Bob, and I have developed a handful of helpful resources—sort of a *Happily Even After* toolbox. I hope you will check out the following and use them if they are a good fit for you:

- the *Happily Even After* podcast series with Bob and Dannah Gresh
- in-person coaching with Bob and Dannah's team at the Pure Freedom Master Class (you can learn about the upcoming dates and speakers at dannahgresh.com)

For now, though, all you have to do is turn the pages of this book.

The first two parts are designed for you to work through on your own, to help you stabilize your heart and prepare for the work ahead of you. Oh, I wish some of the people we worked with had realized how much I needed that *before* I entered into the work of forgiveness and restoration with Bob!

But the time to work on your relationship will come.

The third part is designed to help you as you enter into communication with your husband (if he is willing). You can listen to the podcasts with him to facilitate conversation. Ideally, you'd have either a support group or a counselor in place by the time you get to that section.

And be sure to check out the bonus content at the back of the book. It addresses common questions I receive from women when I speak on this topic—practical questions about finding support and the emotional side of your journey. I hope these will not only help you find answers you need but also remind you that you are not alone.

Other women have navigated these painful waters and come out on the other side. Including me!

I'm here for you as you believe in God to redeem your marriage!

"Fear not, for I have redeemed you;
I have called you by name, you are mine.
When you pass through the waters, I will be with you;
and through the rivers, they shall not overwhelm you;
when you walk through fire you shall not be burned,
and the flame shall not consume you.
For I am the Lord your God,
The Holy One of Israel, your Savior. . . .
You are precious in my eyes,
and honored, and I love you."

—ISAIAH 43:1–4

part one

Your Redemption Story
Is Not Over

It might feel like your life as you once knew it is over. But
there is a brave and sacred route to experience healing for
yourself and your relationship: *redemption*.

Faith is a refusal to panic.

—Martyn Lloyd-Jones

chapter one

We Are Happy Even After

"So if the Son sets you free, you will be free indeed."
—JOHN 8:36

You never forget the day that blows out the flame of happy in your heart.

That afternoon I was at home, waiting for my husband, Bob, to come pick me up in his big red truck so we could "eat our way" through the Centre County Grange Fair. It's a family tradition that sticks better than the fly tape in the pig barns, which are ironically located just next to the Scott's Roasted Pork stand.

Bob was late, but I wasn't mad. In fact, I was feeling really good about my husband that day. A week earlier I'd injured my back helping a friend move. I did not like the pain, but the attention and care my man had lavished on me was another story. He'd been so loving as he nursed me through recovery.

I decided to get in another stretch and was hanging upside down over an exercise ball when Bob walked in.

"Yay," I exclaimed as he sat down in one of our red leather chairs.

I plopped myself right side up and balanced over the rubber orb like a teenager hanging out with her boyfriend. My heart was carefree and unbraced for what was coming.

Bob studied me with a smile. I felt so seen in that moment.

But wait—that look in his eyes was oddly distant and hollow. Empty.

I had recently confronted Bob about my suspicions that he was not walking in sexual integrity. He had blown me off. Now everything in me suddenly realized that he was about to tell the truth. I stood up, moved to sit in our other red chair, and turned to face him.

My counselor and I had been praying for God to work in Bob's heart. I still wasn't prepared for what came out of his mouth.

"I don't know how to find my way back to you or to God without breaking your heart," he began.

And then he did.

He broke my heart.

I am not going to share the details of what Bob told me that day. Suffice it to say that before we were married, my husband had humbly confessed a fierce battle with sexual temptation that we thought would just go away after the wedding. It hadn't. And we'd fought hard against it. Together. For many years my husband had experienced freedom. But one day, sitting in our red chairs, Bob confessed again. He'd lost ground.

It's my decision not to tell more. But Bob wants you to know that what he did is worse than you may think, but not as bad as you might imagine. In his opinion, this ambiguity is another consequence of sin. We both believe that the pain of betrayal in marriage is similar whether a man has looked at pornography, had an affair, or acted out sexually in any of a number of ways.

And yet despite the pain of that betrayal, I am here to tell you that the story of Bob and Dannah Gresh is *not* over.

That sentence is an admission. Writing this book is difficult for me because my husband and I have so far to go—and we know it. *Our story is not over.* Period. Sobering fact.

That sentence is also a battle cry because Bob and Dannah Gresh have won over and over again. *Our story is not over!*

And that sentence, finally, is an exclamation of triumph because the two of us, with God's help, have won over and over again. Our story is not over! Exclamation point. Sublime expectation.

Everything started so beautifully. On our wedding day we made a covenant before God to be united in marriage. We believed then—and believe now—that for Christian couples this is a sacred act with a special purpose. Marriage helps tell the story of a much greater love. It invites the world to see the sacrificial, unconditional love Jesus Christ has for His bride, the church (Ephesians 5:31–32).

It is sacred for you too.
That's why you hurt so deeply right now!
The ache in your heart to know and be truly known
is from God.

At our wedding, Bob and I wanted all our friends and family to know that we wanted to help tell the story of God's love with our marriage. So we decided to speak at our own wedding.

I chickened out, terrified of speaking in public!

Bob did not. The words he shared that day were my favorite part of our covenant ceremony. I delighted to hear them, and I believed we would portray God's love beautifully together.

But we did not ride off into the sunset.

In fact, we weren't even successful at riding off in Bob's new Nissan Sentra. We could not find his car, which the groomsmen had parked for us, in the parking garage after the wedding reception. What a pair we were, walking through each level of that concrete maze—I in my wedding gown and Bob in his tux! But nothing could have stolen the joy of that enthralling beginning.

Of course, our story contains a day that was as sad as that first one was joyful. A day when I had to absorb words I did not want to hear—that my husband's hard-fought battle against lust had become unmanageable. And both our hearts would be bloodied in the aftermath.

Were we still telling the story of God's love?

It sure didn't feel like it then.

It felt like our story as we knew it was over. Or at least the ability to live happily had ended.

But God in His rich grace was not lifting His providential pen from the page, ending our story abruptly. Instead, He was preparing to write a chapter that mercifully revealed something Bob and I could not even see.

We actually weren't as happy as we were pretending to be.

Making a Lie Our Refuge[1]

Many centuries ago, God's special people (the Israelites) went looking for "happy" in all the wrong places. They slid slowly into sin and rebellion. Eventually they made alliances with their enemy the king of Assyria rather than trusting in and obeying the one true God. The prophet Isaiah gave this explanation for what happened over the course of time:

> "We have made a lie our refuge
>   and falsehood our hiding place."
> —Isaiah 28:15 NIV

This describes all too well the circumstances that result in many couples sliding ever so slowly from a healthy covenant marriage into unwholesome, just-living-together misery. They slither into falsehood one small decision at a time over the course of years. And before they know it, they're faking a relationship. Disconnected from God and each other, they just go through the motions. They have made a lie their refuge and falsehood their hiding place.

That's exactly what had happened to Bob and me. We were enjoying our family, going on vacations, managing a little hobby farm, and running two successful ministries. We lived something that *looked* happy. But over the course of a few years we had fallen into something unhealthy and lonely.

My husband was haunted by guilt and shame from sin, which he desperately wanted to overcome without hurting me. And I just had a sense that something was "off" but didn't like the idea of what it might be.

We both felt the nudge of God's Spirit to slow down and get honest. But we didn't.

We just kept on making a lie our refuge and falsehood our hiding place.

Is it possible that you have too?

It is Satan who writes these stories of bondage and destruction in our lives. And he uses only one language: *lies*.

> "The devil . . . was a murderer from the beginning, and does not stand in the truth, because there is no truth in him. When he lies, he speaks out of his own character, for he is a liar and the father of lies."
> —John 8:44

All lies originate with Satan, including the ones your husband may have told you or lived and the one you've been living with him, knowingly or not. The enemy's ultimate goal is your destruction.

But you and your husband do not need to be one of the devil's casualties. God wants to write a freedom story with your life.

> ### *This book is your invitation to make God your refuge (Psalm 46:1, Psalm 91).*
> ### *And His language is Truth.*

The Truth Will Set You Free

Now, maybe the idea of hearing the whole truth from your husband terrifies you. Here again Satan likes to lie to us, telling us that the truth will be too devastating. But truth, though not always pain-free, is never destructive. It always sets us free.

So Jesus said to the Jews who had believed him, "If you abide in my word, you are truly my disciples, and you will know the truth, and the truth will set you free."
—JOHN 8:31–32

The kind of Truth I want you to know is not a set of facts, though the details do matter and will be part of your journey. The Truth that will set you free is a person. Jesus said, "I am the way, and the truth, and the life" (John 14:6). True freedom is found in a living, loving relationship with Him. As you abide in the words of the Bible, you'll come to know the Truth more deeply than ever before and experience a whole new level of freedom.

You might be saying, "Dannah, I have already been set free by Christ. But something didn't work, or I would not be sitting here in absolute misery." Ah, did you forget the part about the epic battle between good and evil? The moment you discovered the freedom of

> ## find Jesus
>
> If the concept of a relationship with Jesus sounds new to you, please turn to bonus content at the back of the book. In it I answer some important questions, including **"How do I know if I'm a Christian?"** (question #1). Getting to know Him is an important step for you to experience the full potential of healing as described in this book.

Jesus Christ, Satan put you in his crosshairs. In this case, your marriage is the target. He wants to see if he can steal what's already yours.

Tell him no!

Plant your feet firmly. You need not let yourself be caught again in the shackles of spiritual bondage (Galatians 5:1).

Remind the devil of the words of Jesus Christ: "If the Son sets you free, you will be free indeed" (John 8:36).

That's not to say that this journey we are about to embark upon together will be easy. It won't be. I know you're probably sitting there downhearted, angry, frustrated, and disappointed with your husband. You could have hard questions about your own culpability in these horrific circumstances. You may also feel defensive and distracted from the work God wants to do in your own heart because people all around you have opinions and you don't know what to do with them.

Been there, done that, as you'll soon see.

But today is the stuff healing is made of, my sweet sister. Cozy up. I'm here to share my heart with you and deliver a fresh download of faith for *your* story.

Here's the most important thing you need to know right now: *you cannot do this alone.* No one experiences the grace of God's redemption power in isolation.

the truth you need 〉 *You cannot do this alone.*

Today I'm writing to you from a historic inn—a Quaker farmhouse just outside Philadelphia. It was built in the 1700s and surely has stories to tell—including a whole chapter about when it was a safe house for the Underground Railroad.

You probably know that the Underground Railroad was not a railroad at all but a complex network of secret routes, churches, privately owned homes, and fearless individuals who aided runaway slaves on the dangerous journey from enslavement. Pennsylvania, a free state just north of the Mason-Dixon Line, provided many entry points into freedom for these desperate men and women.

I pray that this book provides that kind of entry point for you on your journey to freedom! When there has been a great enslavement in your marriage, you face a grueling journey to move away *from* the bondage of sin and pain to the freedom your soul longs to know.

Do you know who led most of those slaves through those secret routes? Those who'd known intimately the pain of slavery but refused to stay in bondage. The leaders were men and women who'd traveled the secret routes themselves and knew the way out.

Bob and I are familiar with the secret, rocky footpaths to freedom and redemption in marriage after the pain of hiding in lies and falsehood. We want to show you those secret routes. We have chosen to be honest with our story so that you can know the Truth and experience liberty.

Imagine closing this book having replaced all the heartache you're feeling with true freedom!

- freedom *from* the blinding pain
- freedom *from* those haunting memories
- freedom *from* hopelessness and confusion
- freedom *from* bitterness and anger
- freedom *from* the opinions people have about you and your marriage

But we won't just be running from the past! The freedom Christ brings is so much more complete than that. We'll be chasing down some things that may be missing from your life right now. So you'll experience not only freedom *from* the things that bind you up and hold you back but also freedom to dive into the future with joy.

- freedom *to* forgive *fully*
- freedom *to* enjoy life and maybe even your marriage again[2]
- freedom *to* make decisions and stand confident with your head held high
- freedom *to* love—again
- freedom *to* turn this hard thing into a purpose so meaningful that only God can see it right now

Even as I type those words, I feel such a stirring in my belly because I know this is true. Why? Because I'm experiencing happily *even* after Bob and I once lived in bondage. When we stopped making a lie our refuge, we discovered that Truth really does set you free.

As I write the first chapter of this book, Bob and I are here at this lovely place called Sweetwater Farm.

Smelling flowers.

Quite literally.

This region of the country has just emerged from a winter that was punctuated by extreme cold and excessive snow. But yesterday, when we walked the grounds of the farm, I noticed the tiniest promise of a much-anticipated spring. There it was—one little crocus bud begging for the sun to shine upon it so that it could bloom. And then another. And another. More crocuses than I've ever seen in one spot, just waiting to bloom.

I began to hope it would be sunny and warm enough for those little buds to open before we checked out of this special place. Then I checked the temperature. It was only just a couple degrees above freezing and not expected to warm up much.

Every now and then I throw up an audacious prayer. No one *needed* those flowers to bloom. I just really wanted them to. *Lord, bring us unexpected and unseasonable warmth—oh, and a bright sun shining all over this field tomorrow!*

We returned to our room and enjoyed the evening. And today we woke to the kind of day that makes us draw suns with smiley faces on them. It's sixty-four degrees in spite of what the weatherman predicted!

Bob and I walked out to see the crocuses. Sure enough, they were open. And to our delight we found another wonder—a whole swarm of honeybees. They were busy as, well, bees. The sound of their buzzing seemed to be a joyful song of praise to God for their first harvest of the season.

We sat down together in the middle of it all—hundreds if not thousands of crocuses and bees. We were just enjoying life together.

And that's the real miracle on this page.

Not that the weather warmed so I could see honeybees on crocuses, but that our hearts have been warmed. To our marriage. To one another.

We are living in happily even after.

And I want to help you experience that too.

Let's get started, my friend.

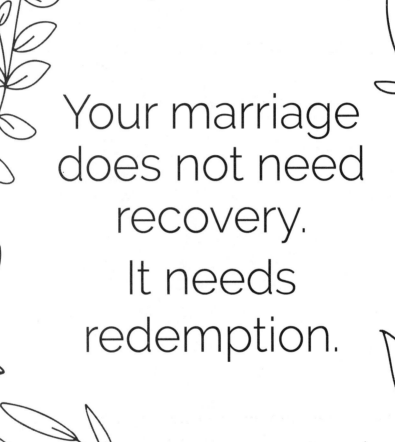

Your marriage does not need recovery. It needs redemption.

chapter two

Can *You* Be Happy Even After?

May the LORD answer you in the day of trouble! . . .
May he grant your heart's desire
and fulfill all your plans!
May we shout for joy over your salvation,
and in the name of our God set up our banners! . . .
Some trust in chariots and some in horses,
but we trust in the name of the LORD our God.

—PSALM 20:1–7

I was walking through my living room when I suddenly had an overwhelming urge to pray for my husband. It had been just a few weeks since we'd sat in this very room, perched in our red chairs, and he'd told me things I did not want to hear.

I dropped to my knees.

For many weeks I'd been struggling to intercede, but now the words erupted from me for a good twenty minutes. I sensed a strong battle in the spiritual realm.

I wondered what was happening in Bob's day.

Almost immediately after that "red chair" session, he had flown to another part of the country to participate in an extremely well-regarded therapy program. But in recent days I had begun to grow concerned about the quality of what he was experiencing there. Many of the faith-based services we'd been told would be available weren't. And though the facility's website had specified support for partners and families, I could barely get them to return my phone calls, let alone schedule the in-person couple's weekend we'd been promised.

Oh, Lord, I don't like not being a part of this! Is that me just being discontent, or is that You redirecting us? Please show me if it's okay to change course. Show Bob!

The flow of words stopped as suddenly as they started.

Well, that was unusual!

I jotted the time down in my prayer journal: 6:51 in the evening. I intended to ask Bob what was going on when I was praying.

Hours later he called.

"Baby, I don't know what you're going to think about this," he began. "But I think I need to leave this place."

He went on to explain that earlier he had attended a specially called meeting. Several of the men in the program had been concerned that their wives were not getting the support they needed. When they expressed their concern, they'd been told they were experiencing "impaired thinking." The therapist had asked them to all repeat, "The team loves your wives and is doing their best to care for them."

I jotted that remarkable statement down. In my experience it was not true. Then I asked, "What time did this meeting happen?"

It was underway at the exact time I was compelled to pray.

You are in the middle of a cosmic spiritual battle of epic proportions. Don't for one second forget that Satan is after your marriage and your man!

You must act quickly.

And with great discernment.

You will need help—good, solid, wise help. And finding that help can be tricky.

The sad state of our culture has resulted in a recovery industry that doesn't always get it right. Never be afraid to change course to find what works for you. And do not let anyone gaslight you.

> Not the cultural voices that seek to normalize sexual sin.
> Not your husband if he tries to defend his behavior or tell you you're overreacting.
> Perhaps not even a well-regarded, "gold standard" recovery clinic.

One reason I'm writing this book, in fact, is that Bob and I did not get our own marriage work started on the right foot. I desperately want to help you—so you won't have to learn the hard lessons I did on the hot pavement of life.

How I wish I could come knock on your door and just listen to your heart. Sometimes you desperately need someone to hear your story and tell you that this is not the end. It's been my tremendous pleasure to be a listening ear for a whole lot of girlfriends who are where you are right now. So many of us have been wounded by our husbands' battle with lust!

Recently one of my favorite friends wrote to me. She recalled that I came to visit right after she discovered her husband's sin. She was so overwhelmed and hurt that she doesn't remember much about those first few days.

But she does remember my visit.

I remember you showing up at my front door with a bag of your favorite granola. (Do you remember?) You came in and listened to my story, my thoughts, my emotions. (I was all over the place!) But I knew you understood. You extended so much grace! I knew you would eventually encourage me to lean into what God's Word would have me do next, but you mostly just listened. You made time to be there with me—you chose me— when I felt terribly rejected, abandoned, and unlovable.

Do you feel rejected, abandoned, and unlovable?

I understand. I have felt those hopeless emotions too.

You might be wondering if there is any hope to be had. The answer is an unquestionable, unequivocal yes!

Pull out some of your favorite granola and maybe a cup of hot tea. Let's sit quietly together as you work through this book. If you need to stop to yell or cry, it's okay. When you just need to stare at the wall for a while and process, I'll be here waiting for you.

In the pages ahead I'll give you a chance to process some of your story. For now, how about if I share a bit more of mine.

When Bob and I found ourselves at relational ground zero, we made the decision to restore our marriage together.

"Get the best help that exists," said a friend.

We did—or we thought that was what we were doing. We both assumed that Bob needed to go into "recovery," so our choice was to invest in one of the most popular types of programs in the recovery marketplace. According to our research, it was a top-notch, "gold standard" program. Although the approach was essentially secular, we were assured that it featured a faith-based track consistent with our Christian beliefs.

But halfway through the forty-five-day program we both felt uneasy. Bob would tell you that some of what he experienced was helpful, but that the presence of God seemed to be roadblocked. The faith-based track we'd been promised kept getting delayed because "the book didn't arrive." And the family therapy weekend kept being canceled, preventing us from entering into the work of recovery *together*.

We had tried to access the best of the world's treatment while integrating it with our Christian faith, but it just wasn't working.

Many women come to me because they have made similar mistakes. Often they turn to whatever local program or therapist their insurance pays for or is most affordable. Sometimes they find a well-meaning pastor to counsel them who does not understand the clinical complexities of what they are experiencing. Other times they find a clinically informed provider who simply does not understand the spiritual battle taking place. Inevitably they find themselves at a place where what they're trying doesn't work.

It can be daunting to filter through who you can trust to guide you on this tortuous journey.

So let me be direct and tell you why the world's recovery marketplace isn't where you want to shop right now. These programs have a terrifyingly high failure rate. The late Neil Jacobson, a professor who specialized in research about marital discord, claimed that just 35 to 50 percent of couples in marital therapy saw improvements and that after a year less than half of those couples retained the benefits.[1] This led John Gottman, a psychologist who has worked for more than four decades on divorce prediction and marital stability, to write that "in the long run, marital therapy did not benefit the majority of couples."[2]

If you place your trust in therapy and recovery, you may find yourself deeply disappointed in the results.

Let me suggest a braver, deeper, more sacred route.

the truth you need *Your marriage does not need recovery. It needs redemption.*

Redemption is the act of being saved from sin, error, or evil and restored to healthy functioning. It's sin that's gotten you where you are. You are probably deeply hurt by and aware of your husband's sin right now, aren't you?

The sad truth is, no program, plan, or psychological treatment will be sufficient to redeem your husband, you, or your marriage. There may be some instruments in the world's toolboxes that God can use to help you, but without Him there will be no redemption. Why?

> There are some things that only God can do, and for us to attempt to do them is to waste our efforts. . . . Among the things which only God can do . . . is the work of redemption.
>
> —A. W. Tozer[3]

No program to heal your marriage will work unless God is at the center of it because He alone can redeem an individual from sin.

The days in which we are living—and so many of our marriages as well—are tainted with the deep pain of *sin*. Of course, most people prefer to speak of the "s" word in hushed tones, if they use it at all. Certainly the black-and-white language of sin is hardly ever used in counseling rooms.

Christian psychologist Mark R. McMinn believes that most of us, Christians included, don't genuinely want to discuss and understand sin. He writes,

> This is not just a mainstream psychology problem; it has affected Christian psychology as well. Philip Monroe, a faculty member at Biblical Theological Seminary, recently noted that only 43 of the 1,143 articles published in *Journal of Psychology and Theology* and *Journal of Psychology and Christianity* have been related to sin, and only four of those are related to the effects or

treatment of sinful patterns. I wonder if we lost the language of sin because the language of psychology took its place.[4]

I wonder too.

The messages of psychological methods, self-help, emotional therapy, and the recovery movement are loud and almost universally applauded, despite their limitations. So it can be easy to forget that Jesus Christ alone has the power to redeem broken people from sin.

I'm here to remind you.

As long as your Redeemer is invited to write your redemption story, there is hope that you can be happy even after your marriage has experienced great pain. But it depends on your answer to this question:

Where Will You Put Your Hope?

Chariots and powerful horses were the racing cars of the ancient world. They epitomized modern living. Not only were they the preferred mode of transport for royalty and the elite, but they revolutionized military warfare tactics.

(I know it seems like I just switched into History Channel mode, but stick with me!)

King David wrote a powerful statement of conviction that we need for a time like this:

> **Some trust in chariots and some in horses,**
> **but we trust in the name of the LORD our God.**
> **—PSALM 20:7**

With those words he was dissing the state-of-the art approach to winning a war—and suggesting that Israel had something much better. They would win, he implied, because they trusted in God's name.

Or, as some versions of the Bible translate it, because they "remembered" the name of the Lord.

I love that.

Because it's so easy to forget.

Recovery programs and self-help books are the chariots and horses of our modern day. They are the world's trailblazing standard in winning mental, emotional, and marital battles. That's why so many in our culture place their trust in them.

But don't be fooled. Don't get spiritual amnesia—not at a time like this!

Instead, I'm inviting you to mindfully put your trust in the name of the Lord. Let Him be your refuge. He *is* the hope you have of redeeming your husband, your marriage, and your story.

In the middle of our marriage work, Bob and I chose to leave that treatment program that is considered the gold standard in recovery. For us it was the wrong chariot because Jesus wasn't driving it.

But this is absolutely crucial: we did not throw the baby out with the bathwater! We have far too much experience to believe the lie that we could overcome the grip of lust in this day and age without the help of individuals who are clinically informed. The same day Bob left that program, he arrived at another one, where a licensed Christian therapy team employed the diagnostic tools and research of behavioral science.

The difference is that they put Jesus in the driver's seat of our healing.

We firmly believe it is *imperative* that you work with a counselor, support group, or treatment program that is both biblically based *and* clinically informed. The next chapter will help you understand why. It contains important information that I wish someone had told me when I began asking the Lord to redeem my broken marriage.

Writing Your Redemption Story

Bob and I are a redemption story in progress. Ours won't look exactly like yours, and it shouldn't. You are a unique couple, and your journey will be different from ours.

There's something our stories probably have in common, though: pornography. Because it's become a sad norm in our culture, it is often the gateway to other marital problems and pain. A 2002 study revealed that among the general public, 68 percent of divorce cases involve "one party meeting a new lover over the Internet," while 56 percent involve one party having "an obsessive interest in pornographic websites."[5] Even more tragically, Christian marriages are not exempt. Did you know that 64 percent of Christian men and 15 percent of Christian women say they watch porn at least once a month![6]

Don't let anyone tell you that pornography isn't harmful. Prolonged exposure to this twisted version of God's good gift dismantles intimacy in a marriage, erodes sanity, destroys trust, and often leads to unfaithfulness.

Because porn is seemingly ubiquitous, many women are becoming complacent about their husband's struggle with it. Do not let that be you. Not *all* men are living in enslavement to a lustful mindset. And the fact that many are enslaved is no reason to simply accept it in your marriage.

You must do something. And you can.

As long as you are walking with the Lord, the Holy Spirit is never going to let you be okay with anything less than complete sexual fidelity in your marriage.

Only God's Spirit can bring your man to repentance, but you can influence your husband to seek the Lord and get the help he needs. Even when a man does not "obey the word" he can be "won . . . by the conduct" of his wife (1 Peter 3:1). You possess that power through Jesus Christ!

I'd like to be a part of your redemption story. I don't have all the answers to your questions. I'm not a trained counselor or expert. I'm just a woman who's been where you are and wants to walk with you a while in your journey because *I desperately needed a friend like that when I was where you are.* It's so helpful to learn from someone who's been there.

For example, it would have been so good to understand what was happening in my husband's brain.

And mine.

So turn the page. And I'll tell you what I wish someone had told me!

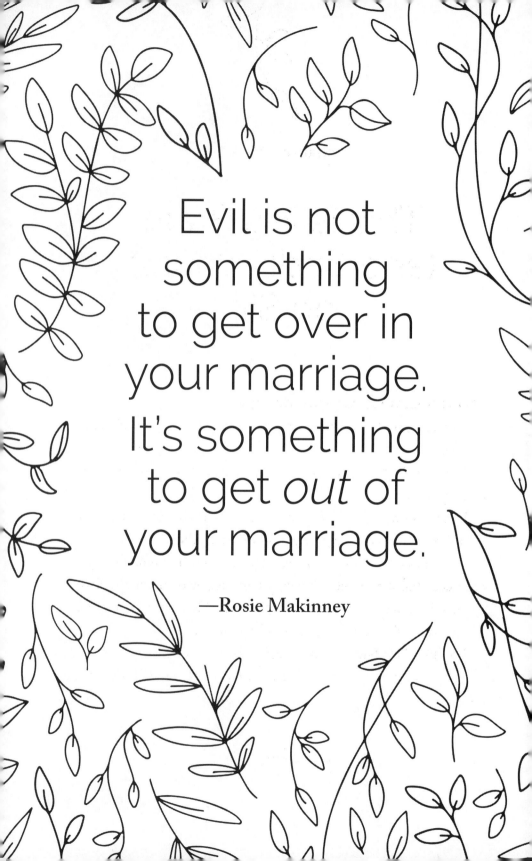

Evil is not something to get over in your marriage. It's something to get *out* of your marriage.

—Rosie Makinney

chapter three

This Is His Brain (and Sadly Yours) on Sin

"Read books on codependency."

So many people told me that. One even gave me a specific book to order.

I ordered it. *Maybe it will be the key to unlock my brain from this prison of confusion.*

With a warm cup of tea in one hand and the codependency book in the other, I began reading, eager for understanding.

As I digested the content, I could see that the symptoms and signs described almost everyone I knew to some degree or another, including myself. And after many years of working with my own therapist, I was pretty confident the diagnosis did not fit me.

I couldn't help but wonder, though: *Am I in denial?*

Instead of gaining clarity, I began to feel more confused than before.

So many of the women I've met whose husbands are caught up in sexual sin tell me they feel confused.

Well, lean in, because I'm about to start giving you your brain back! In the process, I hope to convince you *why* you need *a professional Christian counselor or support group that integrates both a solid clinical understanding of how the brain works and a healthy respect for God's Word.*

Sound overwhelming? Give me a chance to explain. There are three reasons you need (and deserve) this help.

Reason #1: Getting to the Truth Can Be Complicated—and Confusing

I'm glad you are reading this book. Books can be helpful.

They can also end up being super confusing. At least some of them were for me.

The same is true of the so-called recovery movement. Although many of the practices utilized by recovery programs and groups can be helpful, even lifesaving, others bring confusion, especially for the partners of those with a problem.

Case in point: the addiction model for sexual sin.

You've likely heard the term "sex addiction." In 1983, Dr. Patrick Carnes theorized that "out of control" sexual behavior resembled the pattern of alcoholics and that many of them are actually addicted to sex. Thirty years later, though sex addiction is not included as a diagnosis in the American Psychological Association's most recent *Diagnostic and Statistical Manual of Mental Disorders* (DSM-5-TR), the term is widely used today for those who are compulsively using pornography or acting out sexually and seemingly have no ability to quit.

The language surrounding this diagnosis is about as unified as Republicans and Democrats on Super Tuesday. But many people who have faced ferocious battles with sexual temptation do use the term *addiction.* They feel it adequately describes their harrowing experience of trying to stop and being sucked back into their compulsive behavior.

I, personally, approach the term *addiction* cautiously. I do not deny that the addiction model can apply to sexual issues. I've been through too much to think otherwise. But I still have a handful of concerns. And one of them, as I've mentioned, is that proponents of the addiction model traditionally assume that a woman who is married to a sex addict is by definition *codependent* or a *coaddict.*

While that may be true of some women, I do not believe it is true of all women. And I believe this knee-jerk diagnosis can bring unnecessary confusion, guilt, and shame to those who are mislabeled. It can also prevent these women from receiving the specific help they need.

I have support for this belief from a subset of clinicians who recognize strength, intelligence, and maturity—along with suffering—in those who are married to addicts. Some of these clinicians have begun to speak out against the automatic codependent label. A growing number of professionals have started referring to the wives of sex addicts as *partners* instead of *coaddicts.* This has paved the way for important research. There is now strong evidence that the majority of *partners* (maybe as many as 70 percent) actually have symptoms of post-traumatic stress. That's not to say they will be diagnosed with full-blown PTSD, but they experience something similar.[1]

We'll look at some symptoms when we get to Part Two of this book so you can take inventory. For now, I just want to validate that what you have been experiencing is agonizing and also to let you know something important:

Your husband's battle with sin doesn't necessarily make you a coaddict or a codependent woman.

Here are a few things you deserve to hear:

1. **It is not your fault.** You have no responsibility for your husband's sin. None.
2. **You are experiencing collateral damage.** One of the best things you can work on right now is your own healing.
3. **You can heal and grow in any area.** Let God gently use this testing to reveal any areas of your life where He wants to mature you.

I urge you to enter into the future with a willingness for God to use your experience. It may be that any of the terms I've mentioned—"codependency," "coaddiction," or "betrayal trauma"—*could* accurately describe your experience. Maybe all three of them do. But never let someone place a label onto you automatically, without really getting to know you and your situation.

You need support that is *both* biblically based and clinically informed because you have experienced something traumatic and the advice you receive could be confusing. You should not try to deal with the inconsistency on your own, because your brain may not be operating as well as it usually does.

Reason #2: Your Brain May Be Stuck in Alarm Mode

When Ashley Jameson's husband first disclosed his sin, she found herself responding in ways she would have never predicted. Looking back, she describes herself as "irrational." She was even shocked to discover herself throwing things. When she went to someone in her church for help, she told them about both her husband's disclosure and her hotheaded response. She was told, "Lots of women go through this. You just need to forgive."[2]

Telling a woman who experiences betrayal in her marriage to "just forgive" is about as helpful as telling her not to scream when she's dilated to ten centimeters and on the verge of delivering an eight-pound baby. Our bodies do not, thankfully, bring babies into the world every day. But they were designed to go through the painful process now and then.

Your brain is kind of like that. It is designed to worship the Lord, enjoy creation, solve math problems, read books, communicate with friends, and lots of other everyday things. But your noggin was also designed to keep you safe on the rare occasion that it senses imminent danger. When this happens, your brain goes into a unique alarm mode, during which many physiological changes occur. Your brain uses all its energy to protect you.

Within one twentieth of a second[3] a little structure in the brain called the amygdala has taken over, and the prefrontal cortex, which is like the CEO of your self-control, is essentially bypassed. (This explains why you might feel irrational and more prone to yell and throw things.) The amygdala sends signals to the glands that release adrenaline and cortisol, and these in turn affect your heart rate, breathing, vision, ears, blood, skin, and muscles. Everything in you is being readied to fight, run, or play dead.

In most cases the danger passes, and both your brain and body calm down in about a half hour. But that's not always the case with trauma. Instead, your brain may go into a state of vigilance *that doesn't always turn off.*

Don't panic, though. It is possible for individuals with these issues to make strong comebacks.[4] But you do need the help of individuals who have clinical understanding. Your average godly friend at church may be gifted at helping marriages where couples fight about who takes out the trash. That same person will be in over her head when it comes to the impact of your husband's sexual sin on your heart and your body.

A well-trained Christian counselor or clinically informed support group will understand that very important work, like forgiveness, may need to wait. First you need to be stabilized. Otherwise, the important work for your marriage could be premature and incomplete, inevitably creating more confusion and possibly an ongoing trauma response.

If your trauma is new, if you find yourself repeatedly reliving the pain of what has happened to you, or if you are at the point where you fear you can't trust your own judgment, now is not the time for you to worry about "getting past" your pain. Instead, you need some nurturing—mentally, emotionally, and also spiritually. That's why I designed Part Two of this book to help you focus on your own heart and your own brain. But that's also why I urge you to seek help from someone specifically trained to handle the complications of a marriage like yours. Or mine.

Let's look at Ashley's situation. Did she need to forgive her husband? Yes. Did she need to do that while her brain was actively in alarm mode? No.

Thankfully, she got help for her brain and her soul and *then* forgave her husband. Today she guides other women toward healing as director of Pure Desire's biblically based and clinically informed women's groups.

The second reason you need a biblically based, clinically informed support system is that your brain may need some extra care right now. But yours is not the only cranium that's riding the struggle bus.

Reason #3: Your Husband's Brain *Is* Hijacked

If you look at a single-photon emission computerized tomography (SPECT) brain scan of a healthy brain, you'll see that the surface of it will be smooth. But scan a man who is compulsively using pornography or misusing God's gift of sex over and over, and you'll get a completely different picture. The surface looks almost like Swiss cheese—full of holes. It's similar to that of someone who uses heroin,[5] one of the most dangerous and addictive substances known to mankind.

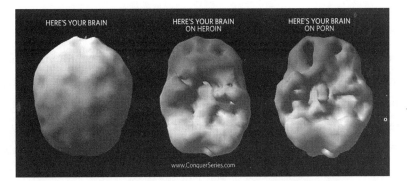

Image Courtesy of Lawrence V. Tucker, M.D., PLLC, Diplomate, American Board of Psychiatry & Neurology and Appearing in the Conquer Series.

The cratering you see in these scans happens because the brain is malleable. This simply means it can be changed and shaped by both physical impact (like a concussion) *or* function (like learning something). Researchers call that quality *neuroplasticity.*[6]

Neuroplasticity means the brain can actually reshape itself to accommodate how we want or need to use it. This is what enables stroke victims to recover and grandmas to strengthen their brains with Sudoku. (Just think about how beautiful that is!)

Neuroplasticity also enables us to keep learning new things. In fact, you can actually see physiological changes when we strengthen a certain area of the brain. For example, one study revealed that taxi drivers in London have larger-than-average *hippocampi,* the part of the brain that helps them memorize and access maps.[7] Kinda cool, huh?

Unfortunately, neuroplasticity also exposes the brain to detrimental changes as a result of experiences like drug use or pornography addiction. Just as heroin or a car accident can destroy the structure and function of a brain, so do the chemicals rushing through a man's head when he is overstimulated by pornography or other forms of compulsive sex. The high comes from *dopamine*, a neurochemical that rewards the brain when we do something that is enjoyable or potentially useful for survival. If you eat a good Krispy Kreme donut? Dopamine! Run a half hour on the treadmill? Dopamine!

Neurochemicals are values-neutral, so the dopamine does its job whether the pleasure comes from something that's good for you—like sex with a spouse—or something that's bad for you—like bingeing on porn.[8] But the way the body produces this reward chemical is different when the form of stimulation is not *intimate* sex, say with a spouse. Neuroscientist Rachel Anne Barr specifies that "porn scenes, like addictive substances, are hyper-stimulating triggers that lead to unnaturally high levels of dopamine secretion. This can damage the dopamine reward system and leave it unresponsive to natural sources of pleasure."[9]

In other words, your husband's brain is chemically hijacked.

What began as a moral problem is now also a brain problem.

Porn also produces phenylethylamine (PEA) and adrenaline. "Fused together, these two chemicals forge an intoxicating sensation which overpowers" the kind of pleasure that can even be experienced with real sex.[10]

So porn acts as a *supernormal stimulus* that can wreak havoc in human lives.

The term *supernormal stimulus* refers to "a stimulus that produces a more vigorous response than the normal stimulus eliciting that particular response."[11] The concept first emerged in the 1950s and 1960s when a prominent biologist discovered he could create artificial stimuli that would override the natural instincts of animals. For instance, he could present an extra-large artificial egg to a bird whose instinct to incubate was triggered by the presence of an egg. The bird would ignore her normal small eggs and incubate the big, artificial one.[12]

Decades later, this discovery enabled a strategy to slow the spread of one of the most destructive insects in the eastern United States. First introduced in the late 1900s to bolster the American silk industry, the gypsy moth attacked our hardwood forests instead,[13] defoliating more than 95 million acres over the next hundred years! But scientists fought back, employing many strategies to combat the problem. One of the most interesting is mating disruption, which involves saturating a specific area with concentrated, artificially produced gypsy moth sex pheromones. Male gypsy moths in these areas become so obsessed with finding the "extra sexy" smelling (but nonexistent) females that they insanely flutter right past actual female insects.[14]

That's what porn will do to a marriage.

I first heard this comparison from Dr. Judith Reisman, a well-respected researcher and opponent of pornography.[15] I became more convinced of the connection when I read an article in *New York Magazine*. The author, concerned over something he observed in his own life, interviewed many men to see if their desire to have sex with their partners and wives was dying because they were using porn.

Turns out he was onto something.

"Over the last decade," reports *Relevant* magazine, "the percentage of American men between the ages of 18 and 30 who reported not having sex in the preceding year exploded from 10 percent to 28 percent."[16] These men are at their sexual peak but don't have any desire for real intimacy—just the *supernormal stimulus*.

And here's the scary thing: it's been predicted that just in the next few years, virtual reality (VR) porn will be a billion-dollar business.[17] When that happens, individuals will be able to interface with a *supernormal stimulus* in a 3D experience that will feel very real. We have no comprehension of the devastation this will cause to individuals and families.

When I said porn acts as a supernormal stimulus that wreaks havoc on lives, I meant it!

Are you beginning to understand that your husband's brain has been radically compromised? He needs help! Don't let him convince you otherwise.

And there you have the third reason you need biblically based, clinically informed support. Your husband needs help from people who understand the complex physiological brain trauma he has brought upon himself through his own sin.

find help

I hope this chapter prompts you to seek out a biblically based, clinically informed counselor, but you may wonder how to find one you can afford. Or you could still have questions about why you need one. Either way, I encourage you to read question #2 in the back of this book: **"Why do I need a counselor (and how can I find a good one)?"** I wrote it to help you avoid some of the mistakes Bob and I made looking for professional help.

Redeeming Our Understanding of Addiction

So far, all I've really proven in this chapter is that you need individuals with clinical understanding to guide you through the technical terminology and rich resources of the behavioral sciences. What I haven't yet mentioned is anything that would require your support system to be Christ-centered.

So let's revisit something I said earlier about the term "sex addiction"—that I use it *cautiously*. One reason for my caution was the tendency to automatically label the traumatized partner of the one who acts out as codependent or coaddicted. But my main concern is that a preoccupation with addiction can erase a healthy understanding of sin.

In the last chapter, we looked at how the language of psychology has partially eclipsed the language of sin. Jay Stringer, author of *Unwanted: How Brokenness Reveals Our Way to Healing*, observes that the same could be said about the language of addiction.

> One of the growing realities in our culture is that we use the word *sin* less and less to describe problematic sexual behavior. The preferred word, if we recognize any disorder at all, is now *addiction*.... This shift is [good in that it forces] us to exchange our intellectual laziness for a more curious engagement with the origins of brokenness. What I'm discouraged by, however, is that Scripture uses the most beautiful and wise words I have ever read to talk about sin.
>
> I believe we need a model that integrates sin *and* addiction. I've found that the more I understand what the Bible says about sin, the more I understand the nature of addiction, and the more I understand what science reveals about addiction, the more I understand the nature of sin.[18]

I couldn't agree more.

Addicts often describe feeling powerless against their behavioral sin. They feel as if they are in bondage to their appetites. Well, I think Jesus would agree with that. In fact, He said exactly that to a group of His Jewish followers who questioned whether they were in any kind of bondage:

Jesus answered them, "Truly, truly, I say to you, everyone who practices sin is a slave to sin."
—JOHN 8:34

Do I have to remind you that we have all practiced sin? (In fact, I've gotten very good at it.) Essentially we have no ability whatsoever to achieve our own freedom from it (Romans 5:6).

The reality is that all of us who have accepted Christ are in recovery from our enslavement to sin. Some are recovering from substance abuse, some from workaholism, some from pride, some from porn, some from gossip, some from slothfulness, some from greed, some from fundamental selfishness. Look around. People in your church are in recovery from a thousand different kinds of enslavement to sin. And at the end of the day, these people are responsible for their behavioral sins, no matter what they call them.

Your husband can call himself anything he wants. You can call him what you want. He is still responsible for his choices and actions. (And by the way, you don't get a hall pass from responsibility if you throw things at your husband.)

The only thing sufficient to buy your husband back from the enemy's grip is the redemptive power of Jesus Christ.

Please do not amputate the work of the Holy Spirit from your box of recovery tools. Satan, the one responsible for our enslavement to sin, is a formidable enemy. You need help from Christian people who are wise about the spiritual disciplines that enable you to access the power of God's Spirit. These are the most important resources you'll put in your toolbox as you and your husband work on your marriage together.

Find Your Team

I am so honored to be a part of your team. But I hope I'm not your only support. After walking through this with my own husband, I am convinced of these four things:

- You and your husband cannot work through what you are walking through alone.
- You need biblical help.
- You need clinically informed help.
- You also need a community of people who love you and are willing to support you (more on that in a future chapter).

the truth you need *You need a professional counselor or support group that integrates both a solid understanding of how the brain works and a healthy respect for God's Word.*

I urge you to build a biblically based, clinically informed support team as you work through this book. If at all possible, try to find a biblically grounded, clinically informed Christian counselor to work with. I realize the process can be expensive, but what's your marriage worth?

The very fact that you're holding this book tells me you value your marriage. And I'm going to assume that you have—at the very least—a bent toward the Truth of God's Word. That means you've got a head start on handling the hardship you're facing now. In the next part of this book, I'll share how to use tools that are most likely already in your hands.

But before you turn the page—you've probably noticed that I like to start a chapter with a short narrative from my own story. I've compiled these from memory using my prayer journal to maintain accuracy as much as possible. That's because I believe radical vulnerability is such an important quality for a thriving community of believers.

Beginning in the next chapter, I'll go back in time a bit to some troubling symptoms I was experiencing before Bob confessed his sin to me. I'm hoping it might help you make sense of some of what you may be or have been experiencing.

"I called on your name, O Lᴏʀᴅ,
from the depths of the pit;
you heard my plea, 'Do not close
your ear to my cry for help!'
You came near when I called on you;
you said, 'Do not fear!'
You have taken up my cause, O Lord;
you have redeemed my life."

—LAMENTATIONS 3:55–58

part two

Equipped for Redemption

God has already equipped you for this trial. In this part of the book I want to help you better understand what you're experiencing and then point your gaze toward five powerful tools you need to participate in God's redemption for your marriage.

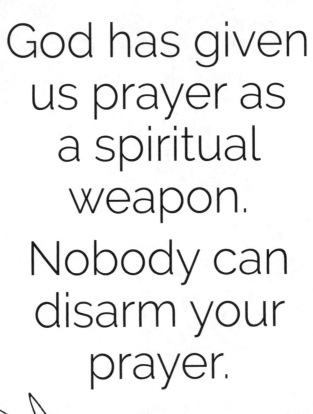

God has given us prayer as a spiritual weapon. Nobody can disarm your prayer.

—Karen Ellis

chapter four

Your Body Feels the Blows . . . but Prayer Is Your Weapon

I opened to my love,
but my love had turned and gone away.
My heart sank because he had left.
I sought him, but did not find him.
I called him, but he did not answer.
—SONG OF SOLOMON 5:6 CSB

Before he told me . . .

My body was in constant pain.

But, according to several doctors, nothing was wrong.

My bones had been x-rayed. My muscles and body tissues had been carefully examined. I'd been tested for everything from Lyme disease to lupus.

Nothing.

It must be in my head, I reasoned.

So I called Tippy Duncan, my licensed Christian counselor and mentor of over two decades. I explained my physical problems and told her that I was also anxious and depressed.

"Is Bob still walking in freedom?" she asked.

"As far as I know," I answered, then confided that he was sullen and angry a lot. So I feared maybe he'd relapsed.

Bob had usually been honest about his struggle with pornography, disclosing his sin to me willingly. Before he proposed to me, he had told me about his temptation and how hard it was to fight. But battle he did, even maintaining his virginity until our wedding night. We both had a very naive hope that having real sex would make the problem go away.

It didn't—because true marital intimacy and lust are two very different things.

Within months of our wedding, we had been determined to fight this thing *together*. We persistently looked for a counselor. After three or four bad fits, we'd found Tippy. For three years she had met with us, given us assignments, gone for walks with us, and loved us. Most important, she had prayed for us and taught us to pray together. God had used her to help us both experience incredible freedom in Christ and connection with each other.

With her help, Bob had experienced extended freedom. But lately, I had to admit, my best friend felt terribly far away. I missed him even though he was living life right there next to me.

"We have to pray," said Tippy. "We cannot lean on our own understanding because we do not have all the information. But God does."

So many women tell me, "I *knew* before I knew."

Either their emotions whispered to them or their intuition screamed at them. And many confide that their bodies told them as well.

Your body processes stress and grief at the cellular level. Sometimes it figures out that something's up even before your brain does.

Unless your husband is psychotic, you will see subtle telltale signs that his life has given birth to the sin of unfaithfulness. For porn. For work. For another woman. For gambling or drink. He may be "working late at the office" a lot of evenings. Or maybe he's been physically in the room with you but not emotionally present. He may be unable to make eye contact with you. Your spirit picks up on these cues, and your body processes them as rejection.

Here's the good news: the very fact that you feel pain and are angry at your husband is proof that your heart has not become too hard to hope again.

And if it just so happens that you are experiencing body pain—headaches, chronic illness, whatever—I have something to tell you:

You're Not Crazy!

Rejection produces serious physical effects in women. There's good science to back me up.

At the saddest end of the spectrum, women who experience divorce are "24% more likely to experience a heart attack compared to women who remain married, and those divorcing two or more times saw their risk jump to 77%."[1] What's happening in their bodies? Research reveals that the stress of rejection causes an inflammatory response in the body. And that's the root of a lot of our maladies,[2] including:

- heart disease and high blood pressure
- chronic pain

- asthma flare-ups
- digestive issues
- frequent headaches
- **joint and muscle pain**
- accelerated signs of aging
- rapid-onset weight gain
- **reduced immunity/frequent colds and viruses**
- anxiety and depression
- some diabetes[3] and different types of cancers[4] that can be linked to stress and inflammation

And it doesn't take a PhD to figure out that mental and emotional symptoms can be a part of the cocktail of confusion you may be experiencing. (We'll look at more of those in the next chapter.)

The presence of these symptoms *is not* undeniable evidence that your husband has a secret sin in his life. There are lots of reasons we may struggle with these maladies. But I'm just suggesting they *could* be linked. A growing body of research suggests the physical pain and problems you experience when a key relationship is not healthy may not be unrelated.

In fact, I'm convinced that many women who experience ongoing battles with unexplained body pain, chronic weakness in their immune system, and mental health issues are experiencing the symptoms of *betrayal trauma.* They just don't know it.

Betrayal trauma is the experience and lingering aftermath of violated trust. When someone you were supposed to be able to depend on—like a parent or, in this case, your husband—does not safeguard you and act safely toward you, you will feel the effect in multiple painful ways.[5] And your body may tell the story even when your mind can't fully comprehend what has happened.

But there is some good news. As you find your voice to tell the story and discover your power to positively impact how the rest of it unfolds, you'll begin to feel relief in your body.

tell me your story

Look at the first few paragraphs in this chapter, including the bulleted list of symptoms, and circle the physical signs and symptoms that may have told you something is wrong in your marriage. I have used a bold font to disclose symptoms I personally experienced when our marriage was facing difficulty.

In the meantime, I need you to know something important and take it to heart. Your current emotional *and* physical sufferings are a part of the grander redemption story God is writing for humanity. They are a result of the sin and suffering of our world and the very reason He has a rescue story in place.

Depression and anxiety.

Chronic pain and inflammation.

Gambling with money or love.

These things did not exist in the Garden of Eden!

Then Adam and Eve rebelled.

There has been sin and suffering in our broken world ever since. Satan has a counterfeit claim on God's magnificent creation, and we feel it acutely.

But before the earth was even created, God knew it would happen and made a plan to buy back what was originally His. He has already made the payment with His Son's life on the cross of Calvary, but He is still at work to completely execute the redemption plan. Until the "day of redemption," we will continue to battle sin and pain (Ephesians 4:30; Luke 21:28; Romans 8:23). For now, we have but a *taste*—a mere deposit— of the complete redemption that is yet to come (2 Corinthians 1:22).

Not to worry. One day we will "acquire possession of it" (Ephesians 1:13–14)!

Until then you and I have the privilege of participating in God's redemptive mission—to take back the ground the enemy steals. And I'm hard pressed to find more important victories to win than those that reclaim our marriages for His kingdom. After all, marriage was designed to be a picture of His love.

How motivated do you think Satan is to see that picture destroyed?

The devil is on a mission too!

Perhaps that's why Jesus said that we would have trouble in this world (John 16:33). The apostle Paul added this to that warning: "those who marry will face many troubles in this life" (1 Corinthians 7:28 NIV).

You know what? Jesus is not as surprised as you are that your marriage is in this difficult place.

Oh, all of that just got very theological, didn't it? Well, I did tell you that I want your marriage to make it. That means you need to roll up your sleeves to gain understanding so you can muscle up your mind.

When a marriage is broken, you've got to work through what you're walking through.

But I *also* want to offer you practical insight, so let's go back to understanding the cocktail of emotions you may be feeling about your husband right now so you can know what to do with them!

Crazy for Him!

Let me try to explain why you may feel confused, crazy, or even physically ill right now, particularly if you don't yet have full disclosure concerning your husband's secret struggles. Imagine you're back in high school again, then consider a few scenarios with me.

In the first scenario, you're playing kickball during a summer rainstorm, and you step on some glass. Your foot hurts, and it's bleeding. It seems a bit worse than something you can handle with the help of the coach. So you head to the ER to get it sewn up.

Simple, right?

Now, in the second scenario, you just happened to pass your ex-boyfriend in the school hallway. Ouch! But you're supposed to be over it, right? The two of you broke up, and there's nothing you can do anyway. There's no ER for your heart.

But maybe there should be.

It turns out that the emotional pain of a breakup and physical pain from an injury operate much the same way in the brain. They share a common "somatosensory representation." That means what is happening in the brain during a functional magnetic resonance imaging (fMRI) scan looks much the same whether there's physical pain from a bleeding foot or emotional pain from a broken heart.

How do we know this? Researchers conducted a study at Columbia University in the city of broken hearts: the Big Apple. No problem finding jilted lovers there. The sad souls were stuffed into an MRI scanner and given two stimuli: a nice dose of thermal pain on their hands, and then a photo of their ex. The brain responded essentially the same way to both types of pain.[6]

This research, first published back in 2011, was the beginning of a growing body of scientific data that suggests romantic rejection does create confusion in the brain. And that uncertainty could be contributing to long-term physical pain disorders such as fibromyalgia and somatosensory disorder. (Not pretty stuff at all.)

But that still doesn't explain why you feel crazy, does it?

Okay, time for our third and final scenario: let's imagine you are that teenage girl who romped in the rainstorm with friends and stepped on glass. But in this case the wound seems superficial—no bleeding, just a bit of a scrape. So you don't do anything about it. But hours later you start to feel fatigued. Someone says you look a bit clammy, and you actually feel chills.

Do you take your temperature? No. You're not a mom. You're a teenager. You wave it off and go to sleep. But the next morning you wake up feeling disoriented and confused. You don't know it yet, but you have bacteria in your body from that superficial wound. You have hours to respond before you go septic. But again, you don't know that's what's wrong, and you don't connect what you're feeling now with what happened yesterday because your wound appeared superficial.

So the symptoms you're experiencing are confusing. You may even feel crazy.

You could experience a similar confusion if your marriage is an incomplete picture—that is, if your husband is engaged in some kind of secret sin. When you don't have all the pieces of the puzzle, the picture of the most important love relationship in your life becomes hard to read. Self-doubt gets in the driver's seat when you cannot see clearly, making it difficult to understand what your body is experiencing. But here's something vital for you to know:

You do not have to stay in confusion if you are a believer in Jesus Christ!

In the next few chapters I want to help you see that God has already equipped you for this trial. You need to use the five powerful tools that I'll tell you about to participate in God's redemption story for your marriage. Here's the first one you need to employ.

the truth you need 〉 *Prayer is a weapon that cannot be disarmed.*

What you're experiencing is not just a physical battle. It's a spiritual one. Even if you're not sure what's going on, you do not have to leave your marriage—or your sanity—to chance. God has given you a weapon to fight the enemy of your soul: prayer. We read about it in Ephesians 6, where we're encouraged to put on the armor of God.

> **Put on the whole armor of God, that you may be able to stand against the schemes of the devil. For we do not wrestle against flesh and blood, but against the rulers, against the authorities, against the cosmic powers over this present darkness, against the spiritual forces of evil in the heavenly places . . . praying at all times in the Spirit, with all prayer and supplication.**
> **—EPHESIANS 6:11–12, 18**

What an invitation from the Lord for when you feel weak or confused. You can choose to rise up in strength to pray at all times *in the Spirit!*

Do you know what that means? It means you have divine help. You do not have to pray in your own strength or understanding because the might of God's all-powerful Spirit will be present in your prayers.

Karen Ellis works as an advocate for the global persecuted church. (Translation: she does a lot of interceding!) She makes this remarkable observation about prayer:

> God's given [prayer] to us . . . as a spiritual weapon. It's not just a nice thing to do. And the interesting thing about treating it as a weapon is, if you think about all the weapons of the world, anybody can disarm you. I can build a bigger nuclear bomb. I can disarm you with your gun. I can take a sword or a knife out of your hand. But nobody can take prayer away from you. Nobody can stop you from praying. Nobody can disarm your prayer. Isn't that a crazy thought? It's an amazing weapon.[7]

You may not have control over your husband's heart or fully understand what's happening to your marriage, but you have authority "over all the power of the enemy" (Luke 10:19). Satan's plan is to use whatever is happening to destroy you, your husband, your children, or even your grandchildren (if you have them). But you can "stand against the schemes of the devil" (Ephesians 6:11) with the weapon of prayer.

And no one and nothing can disarm you!

Sister, prayer is your weapon!

It's Time to Pray!

Beginning with this chapter, I'm going to invite you to intercede for yourself, your husband, and your marriage. I've written these prayers using verses from God's Word. Use some of them or all of them and add your own thoughts as you see fit. But pick up your weapon of prayer!

Father God, my husband and I were united in Your name and have become one flesh. I believe marriage is a profound picture of Your love for Your bride, the church (Ephesians 5:31–32). Right now we are facing many troubles, just as You said we would (1 Corinthians 7:28). Help me to learn what it means to "take heart" and believe that You have overcome even this hardship (John 16:33).

Lord, I am calling on Your name from a deep pit of despair. Do not close your ears as I cry to You for relief in my marriage. Come near me as I call. Help me not to be afraid. Lord, You have taken up my case and redeemed my life. You see me and will help me (Lamentations 3:55–58).

Lord, be my strength. Help me each and every day to put on the armor You've provided so that I can stand against these schemes the devil has brought against my marriage. I recognize that I do not wrestle against flesh and blood, so this battle is not against my husband. Instead, he and I must learn to fight for each other against spiritual forces in the darkness (Ephesians 6:10–12). Help me to pray with full reliance on Your Spirit and to bring before You everything with earnest pleading because it is my great weapon.

In the name of Jesus Christ,

Amen!

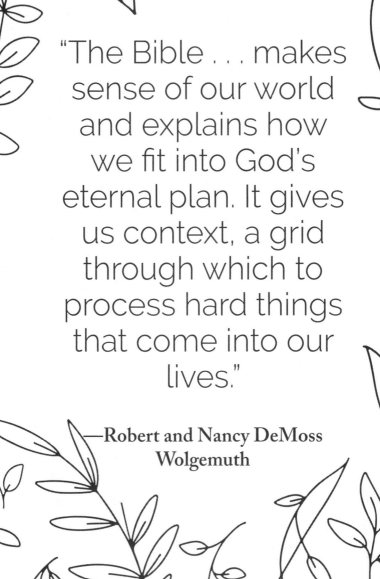

"The Bible . . . makes sense of our world and explains how we fit into God's eternal plan. It gives us context, a grid through which to process hard things that come into our lives."

—Robert and Nancy DeMoss Wolgemuth

chapter five

The Darkness Is Real . . . but the Bible Is Your Light

I am severely afflicted;
give me life, O LORD, according to your word!

—PSALM 119:107

The day Bob broke my heart, I felt dazed and hollow.

I didn't have to say it. Neither did he. Date night was canceled. My appetite for the county fair had been suffocated by numbness.

"That's a lot to process," I said calmly. Almost too calmly. Then I stood up and left him sitting alone in his red chair.

I had to get out of the house.

When I got to the side porch, I wondered where I was headed but tapped the back pocket of my jeans instinctively. *Yep, phone's there.* I headed toward the woods.

When we moved to this magnificent ten-acre farm years before, Bob had asked me never to ride my horse or walk in the woods without it. "I want to be able to come for you if you are hurt," he'd said.

Ironic.

As I stepped onto the overgrown path, I pulled out the phone and called one of my oldest and dearest friends, Donna VanLiere.

I mumbled a bit as I tried to tell her what had just happened. The words didn't come easily.

My dear friend pulled out a verse from Psalm 119 that she'd hidden in her heart and used it to form a prayer over me: "Lord, Dannah doesn't know what to do. You've promised that Your Word would be a lamp to her feet and a light to her path. Would you please use it for her to see her next step?"

The tears finally flowed.

"Dannah," Donna asked, "How much light does a lamp give for your feet?"

I was silent.

She answered for me: "Just enough for the next few steps."

I'm so sorry you're in so much pain. You expected your husband to be someone you could trust, but right now he feels like the enemy. I understand completely. The emotional and physical impact of betrayal is real, measurable, and devastating.

I've cried with, prayed with, and counseled no small number of women who are in your shoes. Women whose marriages were hanging by a thread because of their husband's secret sin . . .

- women whose husbands were actively hiding a growing mountain of debt related to their secret sin
- women who were overwhelmed by their husband's addiction

- women with husbands who either would not or could not keep a job
- women whose husbands were actually living with another woman
- women with husbands who had sexual obsessions so vile that I cannot describe them here
- women whose husbands sent text messages to confess "the other woman"

These were precious believers whose faith was being rocked by the kind of mind-numbing pain you experience when the man you love reveals secret sin of any kind. But I've learned that there's nothing quite as cutting as hearing that your husband has misused God's incredible gift of intimacy. While sexual sin is not a greater transgression in terms of separating us from God, it does tend to have a greater impact in the way it damages us and those we love (1 Corinthians 6:18). No matter how strong we are, it knocks us to our knees.

The women I've spoken with were not weak, frail women, though they were in a season of extreme fragility. They were business leaders, budding writers, energetic community leaders, pastors' wives, children's ministry directors, spiritual matriarchs, hope-filled newlyweds, or vibrant young mothers who'd just experienced an explosion of destruction that took them to emotional ground zero. Strong as their spiritual lives may have been before detonation, now they were experiencing what some consider classic symptoms of trauma:

- **sleeplessness**
- new fears like **claustrophobia**, dread of dying, or abandonment
- nightmares or disturbing dreams
- **forgetting to eat or overeating; extreme weight loss** or gain

- **inability to focus and perform at work or home; inability to read (including the Bible)**
- seemingly unrelated health problems like muscle pain, back pain, high blood pressure, headaches, and even cancer
- extreme or new anxiety
- **withdrawal from relationships**
- **tingling or numbness in the face**
- anger at God
- attempting to control the offending partner or just being in a constant state of **"waiting for the other shoe to drop"**
- panic attacks
- sexual numbness or disassociating (not being really there) during sex with their husband
- being assaulted by mental pictures or images of the offending partner acting out; imagining worst-case scenarios
- freezing up and becoming immobile or unable to respond
- reliving the disclosure or other upsetting events
- feeling extremely helpless or powerless
- suicidal ideation or wishing they were not alive

tell me your story

In the list of trauma symptoms on pages 75–76, circle the ones you're currently experiencing or have experienced recently. I've used bold text to show the ones I suffered in the weeks and months following my "ground zero."

What does a strong woman do when the safest place in her life becomes kryptonite? She prays. Now—I should have told you this in the last chapter, but I didn't have the heart—praying was *really* hard for me. It felt like trying to walk through chest-high mud. My brain struggled to find the words.

When I called Donna, she used the very familiar Psalm 119:105 to form a prayer over me. And it really did give me the energy and wisdom to take the next few steps. I experienced the Word as a light for my path in a very real way that day.

A light for a path doesn't show you the beginning and the end of your journey. And you won't find a single Bible verse that will *immediately* fix everything that is wrong. That's not the promise of Psalm 119:105. The promise is that you'll have the light you need to take the next step.

What a comfort to realize that—and to live in that Truth in the days to come.

After that, as Bob and I stumbled through the next steps in our journey, the Scriptures began to feel particularly alive to me. Over and over God would give "just the right verse" to a friend, who would scratch it on a notecard or send it in a text. And time after time, that verse would give me courage for the next few steps.

I still had difficulty praying, though. But it didn't take me long to figure out that I needed to strap the weapon of prayer together with the "sword of the Spirit, which is the word of God" (Ephesians 6:17).

When I did that, I discovered that the Scripture unlocked my mind to pray and helped me discover what steps to take next.

Your Personal Prayer Tutor

As children we cannot learn to speak unless we are immersed in language. So it is with prayer. We learn it best by being exposed to it. And even during times when we do not know how to pray, we're told to "pray *without ceasing*" (1 Thessalonians 5:17). That means to press in and not stop even when it's hard.

But it really helps to have a tutor. And that's where Scripture comes in.

The Psalms are a particularly good prayer tutor. As an early church father and theologian once said,

> The other Scriptures speak to us,
> but the Psalms speak for us.[1]
> —Athanasius

So if you don't know what to pray at a particular time in your life, the Psalms are a good place to begin. Besides, they're a great comfort when we are, as Psalm 119:107 reads, "afflicted."

We're usually *afflicted* for one of two reasons: either we've been deeply wounded by our own sin, or our hearts are bleeding from someone else's. Again, this is precisely why recovery tools that are not rooted in the redemptive power of Jesus Christ will have limited effectiveness. With our Savior, there's always hope for when we or someone we love are lost in sin.

Lost is the key word. When we are lost, we need direction. And when we are lost in sin, we need a guide.

In Psalm 16 we find David, who is wrecked by his sin, declaring,

> You make known to me the path of life;
> in your presence there is fullness of joy;
> at your right hand are pleasures forevermore.
> —Psalm 16:11

He's declaring his belief that God would show him the direction he needs to go to get out of the dark.

In John 8:12 Jesus said, "I am the light of the world. Whoever follows me will not walk in darkness, but will have the light of life." What a promise! That is *your* confidence.

And get this: Jesus is the Word made flesh (John 1:14). So when you read the pages of your Bible, it is His voice you are allowing to guide you out of the darkness. And, oh, what a Light He is!

Here's why Psalm 119:105 melted my heart when Donna prayed it over me: Jesus was with me in those woods!

In that moment my sad, hard day actually became better than the happy, easy day that came before it. That's when I realized:

Your hardest day with Jesus by your side is always better than your best day without Him.

I hope you will use the incredible power of the words in your Bible to guide you through this hard time. Strap the words of Truth to your prayers and you have a formidable weapon to fight with, my friend! It's a critical tool for a woman who's committed to being a part of God's redemption plan in this world. Here's your second redemption tool:

the truth you need ❯ *The Word of God will teach you how to pray and light your path step-by-step.*

You don't have to be a theologian to experience the power of the Word of God. The Holy Spirit, your sweet comfort and Helper, will teach you everything you need to know. He will bring to your mind and to your praying friends' minds just the right truth at just the right time (John 14:26).

You can rely on the words in your Bible to direct your path, to provide perspective and hope. And wisdom. And anything else you need. Why? Because they are "living and active" (Hebrews 4:12). And they are part of the armor of God we began to assemble for you in the last chapter.

> **Therefore take up the whole armor of God, that you may be able to withstand in the evil day, and having done all, to stand firm. Stand therefore, having fastened on the belt of truth. . . . and take . . . the sword of the Spirit, which is the word of God.**
> **—EPHESIANS 6:13–15, 17**

The Word of God is referred to as the sword of the Spirit. It's the only part of the armor of God that enables us to play offense. All the others are defensive, designed to protect us. But the words of Scripture enable us to take back territory that's been lost.

Friend, you'll need to keep the Word of God especially close for the next few weeks or months. Let me give you a simple way to do that.

When I faced this hardship in my marriage, I bought a set of spiral-bound index cards and began to seek out Bible verses that I could both memorize and pray over my body, my home, and my marriage. This circumnavigated the challenge of finding the words to pray. Each Bible verse would be a light for the next step of my journey. As I faced a specific decision about how to respond to what was happening, I went to God's Word, found a truth I could depend on to guide my next footstep, wrote it on one of my cards, and just soaked myself in it.

I encourage you to grab some spiral-bound index cards or a prayer journal and begin to collect verses that are meaningful to you right now. You might begin by writing out Ephesians 6:10–18. They're precious words of encouragement and power when you're facing a difficult battle. May the Holy Spirit use them to teach you as beautifully and as tenderly as He did me during my season of pain.

I hope you will add to your collection of index cards as often as needed. If you know your Bible well, you can just dig in. If you're not as familiar with it, that's okay. You could just begin by soaking in the verses you find in this book. The more you use God's powerful words of Truth, the more you'll want to use them.

His Word really is a light to your path.

Sister, the Bible is your light in the darkness.

It's Time to Pray!

Since this chapter is about the Word of God being your light in dark days, you might want to soak in the passages that I used to write the prayers below. Strap the sword of the Spirit onto the weapon of prayer and see God at work firsthand.

Lord, I am severely afflicted! That is to say I'm in great pain that has been caused by sin. I feel the darkness of sin and suffering deeply. Please let Your Word be a light for me to know where to plant my feet. May I think of it as essential, the way a lamp is when I'm sitting in a dark room. I commit myself to keep Your righteous rules as I read them and receive them. As I do, give me life as You have promised (Psalm 119:105–107).

Father, help me and _____ to pay attention to each word that we read. When we hear the Bible read aloud, turn our ears toward it. Help us to keep the Scripture in our sight and our heart. I believe that the words of the Bible are life-giving and that they are even able to bring healing to my body (Proverbs 4:20–22).

God Almighty, Your Word is alive and active and relevant to my circumstances. It also can be a scalpel in Your hand, doing necessary surgery to my soul and spirit. Use it to discern my thoughts and the intentions of my heart. May my husband also be willing to have You use Your Word to work in the very marrow of his being (Hebrews 4:12).

In the name of Jesus Christ,

Amen!

Loneliness can be the spark that pushes us to nurture our existing relationships and to make an effort toward new ones.

It can also motivate us to reach out to our Maker with renewed passion and energy.

—Erin Davis

chapter six

You Want to Hide . . . but Community Is What You Need

Two are better than one, because they have a good reward for their toil. For if they fall, one will lift up his fellow. But woe to him who is alone when he falls and has not another to lift him up!

—ECCLESIASTES 4:9–10

The morning after the confession, I woke up only to wish I could sleep it out.

But I couldn't. We had a wedding to attend, and later some guests would arrive from the Dominican Republic.

I trudged into the shower and then dried and styled my hair. Nothing in me felt like putting on a dress, so I grabbed a pair of palazzo pants and an off-white metallic rimmed tank top. They would pass as dressy enough but felt cozy and comforting. I slipped a faux-leaf necklace over my head and grabbed some bangles for my wrists.

"Now for some makeup," I said, trying to talk myself into it. I sorted through my lipstick tubes, looking for the brightest and most powerful red I could find.

Am I really going to spend the day pretending everything is okay?

If you say, "How are you?" to a woman whose husband has just broken her heart, there's a very good chance she'll answer, "Fine."

It's not true. She's not *fine*.

For one thing, she's lonely. And she's feeling lots of other terrible things, including what could range from embarrassment to full-on shame.

These aren't just emotions. They're military strategies of the enemy of our souls. He is weaponizing your own mind to achieve your physical and emotional isolation.

Do not comply.

Loneliness is an emotion we can, ironically, experience most acutely when we are with people. It's not the external state of being away from others. (I love solitude!) Loneliness, rather, is an inner mental anguish.

I experience loneliness most acutely when all is not right in my world, but I feel socially compelled to pretend that I'm fine.

Are you there now? If you're still playing pretend after discovering your husband's sin, you probably know it. Let me help you understand why you're doing it and why you should stop.

Fear Factor

I'm going to make a (very educated and experienced) guess that one reason you're tempted to isolate right now is fear.

People talk. It's a fact.

We've all been around when the gossip mill revs up news about the latest affair. Or when the church leader who confessed to accessing porn gets blacklisted—permanently, with no plan for restoration. Or when friends share opinions and take sides after a couple splits up.

These social experiences might be common, but they are not okay. They create an atmosphere of fear about

- **what people will think about us**
- **what people will say about us**
- losing positions of leadership
- losing a job
- rejection from friends and/or family members
- **the pain and hard work of counseling**
- **how the situation will impact our children** (or grandchildren)
- getting canceled

tell me your story

What are you afraid of? Circle anything in the list of common fears that causes you to pretend everything is okay. I've used bold text to designate how I have struggled.

These concerns are valid. Some items in the list have happened or will happen to you. But my experience is that the fear has to be faced in the right way or it will make matters much worse. Often our greatest fear is about others knowing our secrets. So we hide. But, I beg you, please don't. We need others deeply when something excruciating has happened to us.

And here's something else to consider. If you circled anything you feel you cannot tell anyone, you are probably experiencing shame.

The Genesis of Shame

There was a day when we humans did not have the emotion of shame in our repertoire. Before sin entered the world, Adam and Eve did not feel it at all. Genesis 2:25 reports that "the man and his wife were both naked and were not ashamed."

Shame is an emotion that can only be experienced in a fallen, sinful world. But that's where we live, so we definitely know what it's like!

The first couple responded to this new, acute emotion by hiding from God. And, it seems, from one another's gaze (Genesis 3:7).

We've been hiding ever since. One way we do this is by playing pretend when we feel ashamed.

Shame is a hotly debated term. So let's take a moment to lay a biblical foundation for it. Here's the dictionary's definition.

Shame · "a painful feeling of humiliation or distress caused by the consciousness of wrong or foolish behavior."[1]

Shame is an emotion. And all emotions have a job to do. They are messengers. For example, feeling stressed tells me, "You're doing too much!" If I respond to that feeling appropriately by reducing obligations, the emotion should go away. In this way, feeling stressed is useful if I respond to it appropriately.

So can shame also be useful?

Sometimes. But not always.

Useful Shame Tells the Truth

Useful Shame is the kind we feel when we are acutely aware that we have sinned. This kind of shame is sending us a message that is truthful. For example, a woman may feel ashamed if she cheats on her husband and lies to him about it. *The message of useful shame is telling her that she has a broken relationship with God and her husband. It is an invitation to be restored to fellowship, which is possible if she responds appropriately.*

A prominent sociologist has described shame as an emotion that makes us feel "trapped, powerless, and isolated."[2] But that feeling, horrible as it is, is not always bad for us. When I sin habitually I do feel trapped, as we saw in chapter 3, because I am a "slave to sin" (John 8:34). Sin slaves live separated from God (Isaiah 59:2). So, yes, we'll feel "trapped, powerless, and isolated" if we remain slaves to sin.

But the whole point of the gospel is that we don't have to remain that way. We can allow that trapped, powerless, and isolated feeling to point us toward God's remedy for sin—toward freedom, strength, and healthy relationships.

Too often, though, instead of allowing our shame to point us toward freedom, we respond by hiding—just like Adam and Eve hid behind their fig leaves. I know something about this. As a teenager I was in a dating relationship that became sexual. I felt ashamed, so I didn't tell anyone. A nagging sense of distance from God and others persisted. I really did feel trapped, powerless, and isolated—a slave to my sin.

Thankfully, that did change eventually. The shame eventually caused me to break off a relationship that was terribly unhealthy for me and then to stand before God, confess my sin, and request forgiveness. The painful emotion heralded my restoration with God and redirected me to live in a way that was better. It was a tool God used to help me experience freedom.

And that's always God's goal when He allows us to experience shame. He wants us to respond with godly sorrow and genuine repentance. If we do, "there is . . . now no condemnation for those who are in Christ" (Romans 8:1)!

If we do not do it, however, what once was a useful tool can morph into something toxic.

Toxic Shame Lies to You

Toxic Shame is unrelated to the presence of sin in our own lives. It can manifest when there has been no sin whatsoever. For example, a woman may feel shame when she looks in the mirror and thinks she looks too fat (or too thin). *The message of toxic shame is telling her that **she** is broken. It drives her away from God and others, creating overwhelming loneliness.*

In Luke 8 we read about a woman who suffered from chronic hemorrhage for twelve long and lonely years. She had seen Jesus heal others and longed to receive His touch but was too suffocated in toxic shame to ask Him for help. *What if someone overheard her talking about her embarrassing problem?* She sought to hide in anonymity and decided to just touch the fringe of our Savior's cloak, hoping that would be enough to heal her.

But when this lonely woman touched Jesus' robe, He immediately asked, "Who has just touched Me?" It's a question that begs us to slow down and wonder why the Son of God would need to ask that question. Jesus knew who had touched Him. Did He want her to experience the emotional healing that comes from being seen?

Often when I am advising a woman whose husband is caught in sin, I see very quickly that she is suffering from toxic shame. Sometimes she thinks something like, "My husband would not have cheated if I were more attractive." Or she might believe, "My husband's battle with pornography nullifies my call to ministry." To me these are obvious lies. But toxic shame is a convincing deceiver.

So often these women delay their healing because they spend precious weeks, months, or years pretending and telling people, "I'm fine!"

You're not fine.

Don't hide. You need help.

Here's the irony of hiding: the most common fear associated with shame—whether it is useful or toxic—is being disconnected from others. We imagine that "if they only knew," we would experience rejection and be cut off. So we put on our fig leaves—or our red lipstick. To avoid being rejected, we withdraw and hide by acting like everything is okay. So we end up isolated and lonely, just as we feared.

Think about that!

The act of hiding is illogical and counterintuitive to our fear of being disconnected. When we do not tell others what we are going through, we *guarantee* disconnection. That's when the loneliness sets in and you need to immediately begin to use the third tool of redemption.

the truth you need ⟨ *Community is God's cure for loneliness and shame.*

In the Garden of Eden, God saw Adam's loneliness and declared it was not good. And then He made Eve. And the resulting community of two relieved Adam's loneliness.

Community is an important part of what will cure you too! Let me show why it matters so much to press into the medicine you need.

Something horrible has happened to you, something that created *trauma.* I mentioned *betrayal trauma* earlier, but let's get further educated about it in an effort to equip you to win this battle with shame and loneliness.

Talking about Our Trauma

One definition of trauma is "any disturbing experience that results in significant fear, helplessness, dissociation, confusion, or other disruptive feelings intense enough to have a long-lasting negative effect on a person's attitudes, behavior, and other aspects of functioning."[3] Technically, the word *trauma* refers to the disturbing experience or event. But the way we use it in everyday language really expresses an awareness of the emotional aftermath. So I'd like to use this working definition:

Trauma · "a powerful emotional response to a distressing event."[4]

If the distressing event occurs when someone we love violates trust—that's *betrayal trauma.*

Just last night I was listening to a podcast by my friend Juli Slattery. A Christian psychologist, Juli is the founder of Authentic Intimacy, a ministry devoted to biblically based sexual discipleship. On the podcast she was speaking with an in-demand trauma therapist named Victoria Gutbrod.

I was riveted by their conversation. What they were saying answered so many questions about *why* we cannot process our pain alone.

According to Juli and Victoria, trauma research shows that people who "process" (talk about) their distressing event within the first twenty-four or forty-eight hours tend to experience a successful recovery. But those who are not able to talk freely about what happened are more likely to develop an ongoing trauma response—to be trauma*tized.*[5]

Why?

Because we are designed to need help in processing difficult life events.

As I listened to Juli and Victoria, I discovered that we all need help interpreting what happens in our lives, especially the painful events. (This is especially true for children but applies to adults as well.) Talking about an experience with others helps our brains assign value to it, develop understanding of what happened, and then—here's the key—release the emotion associated with that event. Translation: our hearts let go of the trauma!

It was like a light bulb went on in my brain when I heard that! For years I have been telling people that emotions are messengers. If we respond to them appropriately, they go away. Trauma *is* the emotional response to a distressing event. So of course the messenger will depart once we respond to it! It has done its job. We will probably still have some work to do, and that often takes time, but we can do it in a calmer, less fraught frame of mind.

As I listened to that Authentic Intimacy podcast, Victoria said something so hopeful. Lean in for this one:

> Not everybody who experiences trauma
> is traumatized.[6]
> —Victoria Gutbrod

In fact, for many people trauma becomes a catalyst to develop strength. One study suggests that "nearly half" of trauma survivors experience post-traumatic growth, defined as "positive psychological changes after encountering challenging events."[7]

You do not have to live as a victim just because you have experienced a terrible event. You can have victory over this pain and shame. This bad memory can become an event of the past, not a forever hurt. Those who talk about what happened to them truthfully and honestly in the community of safe individuals are the ones who tend to experience emotional recovery more quickly.

Finding the Community You Need

How does all this apply to your situation?

Well, first: I hope that your husband is experiencing useful, godly shame! Hopefully it will lead him to confess his sin to God, to you, and to some godly men in his life. A key component of restoring your marriage is your husband's humble, authentic repentance. It may be difficult for you to watch your husband experience this. I encourage you not to interrupt it with words of comfort that minimize his win. Let God's Spirit use his emotions to draw him to real repentance.

The Bible supports this approach. It is full of verses that communicate our need to help each other when we are battling sin and shame. But they tell us to "put away falsehood" and "speak the truth" (Ephesians 4:25). There's a proverb that teaches us that concealing sin is hurtful but that we "obtain mercy" when we speak honestly about it (Proverbs 28:13).

Your husband was "caught" by his desires. Now the body of Christ has a work of restoration to do in him. And that takes a community—a team of godly men to do the work of restoring him gently.

But here's the second thing I hope you get out of this chapter: *you need community too.*

It is quite possible that you're being assaulted with some undeserved toxic shame. Your husband's sin is not your fault, and you have nothing to be ashamed of. But the reality is that his sin and his shame have probably impacted you deeply.

So what should you do with *your* suffering?

Tell someone. Resist the urge to hide, to pretend that everything is fine.

Do it even if your husband will not.

You need a community of godly women to restore your heart.

Women like Rosie Makinney.

find your friends

I encourage you to take advantage of the bonus content at the back of the book. Question #3 addresses the question, **"Where can I find free or affordable support groups?"** It directs you to some helpful online and in-person group therapy options.

Just eight days after Rosie married her husband, she confronted his pornography problem. Can you imagine? Prior to becoming a Christian she'd been in a "long-term" relationship with a man she refers to as an "unrepentant porn addict." So she was "well acquainted with the all-consuming mistress of porn, [who] had her hooks deep" in Rosie's new, Christian husband.[8] She confronted him and required him to get help. He did. But Rosie knew she needed help too.

In the beginning, Rosie didn't have any people, but she's a resourceful woman. Her husband, Mark, *did* have a support group as he worked toward recovery for his pornography habit. So she typed up a note, printed it, and gave it to him to hand out in his weekly meeting:

> Hi, my name is Rosie, and I am a wife of a man who attends the same group as your husband. It's great that our husbands are getting support, but sometimes I wish that I had support too. I would love to be able to chat with someone else who "gets it" and wondered if you felt the same. I was thinking of hosting a little informal get-together at my house next month. Is this something you would be interested in attending?[9]

That was the beginning of an entire network of support for women in her state. It has burgeoned into a Facebook group that ministers to women in more than one hundred countries. Today Rosie's husband lives in freedom, and she runs a budding new ministry called Fight for Love. It helps women whose husbands are using pornography get educated, get connected, and get help.

I hope you'll find your friends. And they really will be that to you, even if they begin as strangers.

When I was looking for women to support me, I discovered that there were two types of community a hurting wife needs.

- **You need friends who have worked through or are working through what you are walking through.** It's so healing and helpful to be able to communicate with women who have been where you are. They will understand your unique journey. There are lots of support groups already available (in person or online), or you could develop your own like Rosie did.

- **You also need to let your closest, safest existing friends know what you are experiencing.** It is my opinion that the greatest way to break through the toxic shame is to tell women who already know you and love you what is happening in your life. It's one thing to tell an author or speaker or another woman in a support group who barely knows you. That's helpful, but it doesn't always break the bondage of toxic, undeserved shame. Sometimes you need a girlfriend who truly knows you to look you in the eyes and simply say, "I see it all, and I'm here for you."

It probably should go without saying that you should use prayer and discernment as you decide who to let into your inner circle of confidence. There's a big difference between sharing your pain with a trustworthy friend or a confidential support group and broadcasting your troubles (and your husband's sin) on social media. There's also a lot of gray space in between those options, so it can be difficult to know what to say and when to say it. But the Spirit will guide you if you let Him. Actually, you will need God's Spirit in all of these conversations because they require great courage! If you are unsure where the boundary lines are or if you're in a situation where someone close to you tends to gossip, seek out a counselor or a confidential support group *first*.

One more thing: your support community needs to be made up mostly of women *who share your faith*. Make a point of surrounding yourself with people who have experienced the redeeming love of Jesus. The conversations will be different. Richer. Deeper. More useful.

More important, your own faith will be bolstered.

Your Shield of Faith

Now let's look at an important part of the "armor of God": the shield of faith.

> **In all circumstances take up the shield of faith, with which you can extinguish all the flaming darts of the evil one.**
> **—EPHESIANS 6:16**

Years ago I studied the Roman military armor that Paul would have had in mind when he wrote this passage. I learned some fascinating things about the shield the Roman soldiers carried. It was large—about two by three-and-a-half feet. Crafted of curved wood, it was often covered with a layer of leather that could be soaked in water. This was the secret to putting out flaming darts or arrows.

Imagine holding a shield that large up to protect you. It would get heavy quickly.

Unless you had help. The kind of help that comes from a community of faith.

Another interesting observation is that flaming darts tend to come from above. To protect themselves the Roman soldiers often clustered together in a kind of "turtle" formation. Those in the middle held their shields above their heads to create a roof above them. Soldiers to the outside of the cluster held their shields up to make a wall. When they worked together, they were better protected.

Did Paul have that in mind when he referred to our faith as a shield? It's certainly a beautiful picture of how community helps protect us.

Go find your friends.

Sister, community is your cure for loneliness.

It's Time to Pray!

Can I encourage you to pray *with* someone? This is the perfect time to invite a godly friend into your prayers for your situation. Just text her and say, "Let's have coffee. I need a prayer partner." Then do it and bring the prayers below when you meet.

Lord, I am lonely and afflicted. My husband's sin has wounded me deeply. Turn to me and my need with the fullness of Your grace. Relieve me from the troubles my heart is experiencing and free me from this anguish. Take away my own sin. Guard my life and rescue me. Do not let me be put to shame. I'm running to You for safety (Psalm 25:16–20).

Jesus, my husband has been caught in sin. Only You can save a man (Acts 4:14), but Your Word says that those who are spiritual can and should restore him gently. Please send godly men to do this work in his life. And help me to press so deeply into Your Spirit that I am capable of being gentle with him when my tongue wants to react with harshness. Help me to keep a watch on myself so that I do not respond to his sin with my own (Galatians 6:1).

Lord, Your Word teaches us that praying for someone's sick body is fruitful. What about when someone's heart is sick with the impact of sin? Lead me to the right people to pray for my emotions and heal them. Help me to confess my own sin because that seems to be an important step in righteous prayers. I believe the prayers of my community are powerful and effective. Help me not to hide from them (James 5:13–16).

In the name of Jesus Christ,

Amen!

Suffering
provides
the gym
equipment
on which my
faith can be
exercised.

—Joni Eareckson Tada

chapter seven

Your Husband Can't Be There for You . . . but the Lord Is Your Strength

*"Come, let us return to the L*ORD*;*
for he has torn us, that he may heal us;
he has struck us down, and he will bind us up."

—HOSEA 6:1

Exactly one week from the day Bob confessed his sin to me, we were at the University Park Airport, waiting for his flight to a recovery clinic. It was certainly a drastic choice for us, but we felt good about our decision, especially with the promised faith-based track.

So why didn't I want him to go?

"Goodbye," Bob said distantly, as if he were talking to an Uber driver.

He leaned over to pick up his suitcase, and I could see that he was fighting back tears. But he refused to make eye contact with me.

He turned to go.

He looked back, walked toward me, and brushed my cheek with a halfhearted kiss.

It felt like an obligation.

Like a rejection.

Bob says he doesn't remember it that way.

In his mind's eye *I* was the one who brushed his cheek with a halfhearted kiss. He remembers feeling I was deeply ashamed of him that day.

Shame will twist experiences to make you *both* feel rejected by the other.

We've already discovered that shame is a deeply private emotion. We also learned that God can use it as a tool to convict us of sin and direct us back to His heart and the heart of others. In the hands of God, useful shame can be a kind of shepherd's crook pulling us back and then redirecting us to Truth.

But shame is also a favored weapon of the evil one. He uses it in a toxic and twisted manner to dismantle our relationship with God and each other. In the hands of Satan, toxic shame is a bayonet used to force you to run and hide. From God. And from each other.

Your husband is the only one who can decide if his shame will drive him away from people and God or if it will be the tool he allows God to use to redirect his heart. At times he may totter back and forth between useful shame and toxic shame. His battle with shame will prevent him from doing things he needs to do for the good of his marriage, even if he *wants* to do those things.

C. S. Lewis astutely observed this dynamic:

I sometimes think that shame, mere awkward, senseless shame, does as much towards preventing good acts and straightforward happiness as any of our vices can do.[1]

And that's what was happening that day at the airport. Useful shame was the tool God used to put Bob on a journey to go get help. But toxic shame is why Bob couldn't look me in the eye and love me when I took him to the airport. Satan was pointing it at my sweet husband and telling him to run because he was unwanted and unworthy.

As soon as a man begins to express godly sorrow for sin, Satan pulls out his favorite tool to stop the process: confusion.

The enemy of our souls is so double-minded.
He convinces us that sin isn't so bad before we do it.
But afterward he tortures us with our unworthiness
because our sin is so very bad.

It's confusing and destructive to a person's emotional stability.

That's what Bob was struggling with that day. He was trying hard to listen to God and not the devil in the midst of all that toxic shame.

But I didn't realize that. What I felt was rejection. And the hard reality that my husband just wasn't there for me in my moment of deepest need.

His Emotional Straitjacket

So here's the takeaway. Right now your husband is unable to help you with your pain. I know how badly you want him to. I've been there. But he simply can't.

I once described the pain I felt at the airport with a word picture. It felt as if Bob had intentionally driven our car directly into a tree at a high speed. Thankfully we weren't dead, but we were both bleeding. It's just that Bob's side of the car had hit the tree straight-on, so his injuries were more severe. The EMS team that showed up triaged us and immediately went into action, extricating my husband, plopping him on a gurney, and rolling him off to the ambulance. I was left behind, stuck in the wreckage as the lights and siren of the ambulance faded into the distance.

Who was going to take care of *me*?

Not Bob.

He had apologized, and he was deeply repentant about how his sin had impacted me. But my husband was in no condition to help, no matter how much I wanted him to be my hero.

I learned this ever so slowly. And it was our beloved friend Peter Kuiper who helped me finally realize what was going on. He said,

"The one who broke your heart
has no ability to fix your heart."[2]
—Peter Kuiper

Bummer.

Exceedingly very big bummer!

And it doesn't just happen when a husband is about to board a plane to rehab. Many wives tell me that when the shame kicks in, he checks out. Even if he's right there next to you, he's probably not in any condition right now to help you.

But, my friend, there is One who does have the ability to fix your heart. He wants to help you. And He knows exactly what rejection feels like (Acts 4:11; Matthew 8:34; Luke 17:25). He empathizes with you in a way no one on the planet can. And He, unlike your husband, has the ability to care for you right now.

Will you let Him use even your husband's rejection (or seeming rejection) to make you into what Jesus knows you are capable of being?

Put the work of your healing in His hands.

The Role of Rejection in Your Story

Rejection, just like shame, can be one of God's good tools.

We see that so clearly in the life of King David.

Remember, he did not immediately rise to the throne of Israel after he was anointed by the prophet Samuel as a young man. Instead, he had to endure many years of testing and schooling to prepare to serve as king. And one of his more difficult training courses may have been *Rejection 101*.

The reigning king, Saul, consumed by jealousy, chased David into hiding for over a decade. Saul's rejection of him was a divine test to see if David would believe God and walk in the truth of His Word.

David wasn't just rejected. He *was* a reject. And he lived with rejects. The Bible records that "everyone who was in distress, and everyone who was in debt, and everyone who was bitter in soul, gathered to him" (1 Samuel 22:2). David welcomed them and trained them, gradually building an army and a community of families.

And they eventually rejected him too.

It happened this way: After a fierce battle with a people called the Amalekites, David and his men returned to their camp in the town of Ziklag to find it had been burned and looted by the enemy. Every wife and child was gone—taken alive. That's when the man who had been rejected by his king, rejected by his people, and even rejected by their enemies (1 Samuel 27:29) was rejected by the rejects. The men leaned into their grief by blaming David for what had happened. They even talked about stoning him (1 Samuel 30:1–6).

How did David respond to this test during his course work in rejection? Did he tell the angry men, "Hey, I'm hurting too!"? Did he beg them to heal his broken heart? Or argue with them and blame them in turn? Or run off to find others who might commiserate with him?

No.

> David strengthened himself
> in the LORD his God.
> —1 Samuel 30:6

In this vulnerable moment, David reached out to God for strength. He got alone with the God of the universe to strengthen himself. Some Bible versions (notably the King James Version) say that he "encouraged" himself in the Lord. When many would just give in to the sadness, he determined to be strong. And while many would try to draw strength and encouragement from other people, David went directly to God in prayer.

You can do that too. Rejection is your invitation to turn to God for strength.

Will you?

Finding Strength in God

Even Jesus withdrew to places of solitude to pray (Luke 5:16; 6:12). And that's what I'm asking you to do. To get alone with your ultimate Source of strength. It's time to unveil your fourth tool of redemption.

**the truth
you need** *The strength of the Lord will help you get your family back.*

If you have given your heart and life to Jesus Christ, you are His beloved. He desires to strengthen those He loves. Read these words that were breathed by God for His people:

> "I have chosen you and not cast you off";
> fear not, for I am with you;
>   be not dismayed, for I am your God;
> I will strengthen you, I will help you,
>   I will uphold you with my righteous right hand.
> —Isaiah 41:9–10

This is the heart of God. He wants to strengthen and help you. Lean into Him in prayer. Seek direction through Scripture. Surround yourself with Christian community, but separate yourself from the din of opinions—including your husband's—and strengthen yourself *in the Lord*. Here are some ideas that might work for you:

- **Use time at home to be with the Lord while your husband is away.** While Bob was gone I canceled many of my career responsibilities and cleared out my social life so that I could spend large segments of time in prayer with my index cards full of Bible verses. I also used this time to read and learn about the battle Bob was fighting. If the issues in your marriage have resulted in time away from one another for some reason or another, don't spend that time being busy. The temptation will be to medicate your pain with things to do. Resist it. Strengthen yourself in the Lord.

- **Spend a few days alone with the Lord.** Maybe your husband is still at home and the challenges you're facing won't require him to go away for counseling or treatment. Or perhaps you're just trying to diagnose the problem and figure out what to do next. Could you go away for a weekend to be alone with the Lord? If possible, create a time-out in your relationship with your husband so you can focus on your relationship with God even if it's just for a few days. Strengthen yourself in the Lord.

- **Get up early or stay up late to be with the Lord.** Maybe your circumstances aren't the kind that require immediate attention. You're just reading this book to improve some things that need attention in your marriage. Or it might be that your children or bank account don't allow either of you to get away right now. Then you may need to rise early or stay up late each day. When my kids were very small, I had to get up before they did to have time with Jesus. Now I have to get up early to have that time before Bob wakes up. It's so very worth the loss of sleep! Strengthen yourself in the Lord.

- **Use your lunch breaks to be with the Lord.** It may be a job that keeps you from getting away for an extended period. No worries. Your lunch hours can still provide tremendous time for strength training. When I first began spending concentrated time with the Lord each day, I was in my twenties and working full-time. So I met with Jesus during my one-hour lunch break every day at a local park! It worked beautifully for me and could be just what you need. Strengthen yourself in the Lord.

In some circumstances it may be important to take a more drastic step. Because some women need to hear this, I'm going to include it, but please seek the advice of your pastor and a Christian counselor before you execute this option:

- **Under the guidance of spiritual leadership, consider a therapeutic separation.** For your mental benefit and spiritual benefit and the ultimate rescue of the marriage, it may be advisable for the two of you to live apart for a specific period of time. This could be as short as a couple of weeks, but it could be much longer. The goal of a therapeutic separation is not to move toward divorce, but to help both of you pursue individual healing so that the work you do together is more successful.

Whatever you do, I urge you to find a way to really focus on strengthening yourself in the Lord before you begin on the next section of this book and as you work through it.

tell me your story

In the list of options for finding time to spend with God, put a star beside the option you believe will work best for your life. If none of them seems like a viable option, write your own creative idea in the margin. Jot down any thoughts or commitments you don't want to forget as you seek to strengthen yourself in the Lord.

Get Your Family Back!

In case you are wondering, strengthening yourself in the Lord does not result in becoming so heavenly minded that you are no earthly good. After David turned to the Lord in his distress, he was able to respond to what was going on around Him *in the power of the Spirit.* And do you know what he did?

Rather than running from those who had rejected him or lashing out at them, David invited them to remember who they were. He essentially said, "You are husbands. You are fathers. You are warriors!" And then he invited them to act like it.

They went after the Amalekites and retrieved every wife and child. They got their families back!

And that, of course, is your ultimate goal. After you have soaked up the strength of the Lord, He will prompt you to get to work saving your marriage. Hopefully it will be with your husband's help after he has been strengthened in the Lord himself. But for right now I strongly encourage you to resist the urge to go to your husband for comfort or to respond to his need.

Let your husband stand alone before God and get help from godly men.

As for you, take this time to rest in Jesus. Soak in His love. Stabilize your own heart as you get help from prayer, Scripture, and the support of godly women.

I have found that many women skip this important step of restoring their marriages. Rather than tending to their own troubled hearts, they are often swept into the work of caring for their husband or marriage. I'm afraid they have believed the lie that the future of their marriage and family depends upon them.

Only Jesus can redeem a family broken by sin, my friend. Take a cue from David. He did not address the friends who had rejected him, attack the Amalekites, or go get his family back until he *first* strengthened himself in the Lord.

Will you strengthen yourself in the Lord?

Let's look at Ephesians 6 one last time. As Paul nears the end of his letter to the church at Ephesus, remember, he invites them to put on the armor of God. At the top of the list of the description of that armor is this:

> **Finally, be strong in the Lord and in the strength of his might.**
> **—EPHESIANS 6:10**

The armor of God is needed for spiritual warfare and suffering. But those tools mean little without the strength of the Lord.

So slow down. Sit with Him. Strengthen yourself in the Lord.

Sister, the Lord is your strength.

It's Time to Pray!

When I need the strength of the Lord in a special way, I like to get on my knees when I pray. It demonstrates the posture that I hope is in my heart. Perhaps you'd like to try it today.

Oh Lord my God, I feel deeply rejected. Help me not to turn to worldly solutions for this emotion. Instead, I am coming to You, asking to be strengthened in You (1 Samuel 30:6). You have not rejected me. Instead, You have chosen me. What a thought! Help me not to be fearful, but to know that "I Am" is with me. You are my God. You have promised in Your Word that you will strengthen me and help me. You'll even hold me up with Your very own righteous right hand. Do that for me today (Isaiah 41:10).

Hear my voice when I call to You, Lord! Be merciful and answer me when I pray. I will seek You. Please don't hide Your face from me. Even if my mother and father do or have forsaken me, You receive me. Thank You, Lord. Teach me how to walk in Your way through this dark valley. Lead me in the straightest, shortest path through this pain. I'm going to choose to be confident that I'll see Your goodness. Until I do, give me patience to wait for You. Help me to be strong and take my courage from You as I wait (Psalm 27:7–14).

In the name of Jesus Christ,

Amen!

The biggest danger to a happy marriage is idolatry. We forget our true Spouse because our heart settles on a visible human spouse. So single Christians—or Christians who are unhappily married—are uniquely placed to remind . . . us that we are all betrothed to Christ.

—John Newton

chapter eight

You Don't Feel It . . . but Love Is the Remedy for His Sin

The voice of my beloved!
Behold, he comes,
leaping over the mountains,
bounding over the hills.
—SONG OF SOLOMON 2:8

I was home in Pennsylvania, doing phone therapy with Tippy. Bob was in another state for treatment. But he and I were separated by more than miles. There was a wall of hurt and shame between us.

I stared at the list of questions Tippy had given me to answer.

- What happened?
- Why am I here?
- How can this advance God's purpose in my life?

That last question really stung. I couldn't talk about purpose without my mind going back to the streets of Chicago. Bob and I had been on our way to enjoy some deep-dish pizza when words seemed to just plop into my head.

> Your mission is to encourage men and women of all ages to live lives of purity, equip them to heal from past impurity if it exists in their lives, and to experience a vibrant, passionate marriage that portrays the love of Christ for His bride, the church.

We'd rushed to a business center so I could write them down—as if I could ever forget them! They were embedded into my heart as a life calling. But now I realized that the purpose that had meant so much to me through the years felt at odds with Bob's battle.

How can I pursue a mission to help others portray the love of Christ for His bride through their marriages when mine looks like this?

"Dannah," challenged Tippy, "What if that assignment God gave you in Chicago wasn't for you to help *others?*"

She paused as if inviting me to soak in what she was about to say next: "What if God spoke that into your heart so profoundly for you to live out that kind of love in *your own marriage?*"

I answered her flatly: "I don't want that assignment."

I know you probably don't feel "in love" with your husband right now. And maybe, like me, you don't want to do the hard work of loving him through this devastation. I understand. But that's exactly what I'm going to ask you to do next.

Let's get right to the Truth you need.

In full disclosure, this chapter is going to require some deep thinking. But if you'll follow this trail of Truth with me, you'll discover one of the deepest riches of God's redemption.

the truth you need ⟨ *Covenant love is the only remedy for His sin and provides the pathway to redemption.*

God's Revelation of Love

I believe God is our Maker. He created us (and not the other way around). When He made us, He planned for all of nature to reveal His power and His character (Romans 1:20).

Of course, one of the most important qualities about Him is His love. So He placed a visible revelation of it into the world.

And what did God choose to carry the sacred picture of His love? Marriage.

The very thought of that bites when your marriage is a mess. It's easy to believe this lie: *my marriage is not a picture of the gospel.*

tell me your story

Do you believe that your marriage could not possibly be a picture of the gospel? Why or why not? Jot down a few thoughts in the margins before you read on.

My friend, let me introduce you to something that I hope will bring incredible clarity to the way you respond to the difficulties of marriage and try to figure out where love fits into the picture. I'm talking about the concept of *covenant love.* You may recall that I mentioned this kind of love in chapter 1. It's such an important tool for every marriage, especially those facing difficulties.

I began to study covenant love more than twenty-five years ago when I read a book by Kay Arthur called *Our Covenant God: Living in the Security of His Unfailing Love*. That book and others on the topic introduced me to a deeper understanding of the faithful love of Jesus Christ.

Kay asserted that becoming informed about *covenant* helps us to truly "understand the intimacy and intricate details of God's plan and purpose. . . . It frees us to bask in His love and to move through every circumstance of life in the security of His promises."[1]

Couldn't you use some of that security as you walk through what may well appear to be a time of incredible insecurity?

Covenant Language

Covenant is a difficult word for a lot of us to understand since our modern culture has no category for it. But it's an important concept in the Old Testament because it describes the relationship between the God of Israel and His people through the centuries.

When you come across the language of *covenant love* in the Bible, you'll see two things.

First, you'll notice an incredible, possessive intimacy and belonging marking the relationship between God and His people. *My people*, God says. *You are mine*, He declares. My favorite part of the Bible is where it says this outright: *I love you* (Isaiah 43:4).

A covenant is all about love.

Second, you'll see a binding legal aspect to a covenant relationship. It requires both parties to show up with unbreakable faithfulness, and there are dire consequences for breaking a covenant agreement.

A covenant is also about law.

Let's explore the legal ramifications of breaking a covenant by looking at the first place the idea of a covenant shows up in the Bible.

Covenant Consequence

God had promised Abram that his family tree would be so plentiful that each star in the sky represented one descendant. But the older Abram grew, with no children in sight, the harder it became to believe that promise. So Abram asks, "Oh Lord God, how am I to know that I shall possess it?"

In answer, God told Abram to go get some animals to sacrifice.

Now, that would've been exciting news to Abram. The God of the universe was inviting him to practice the very familiar ancient ritual of covenant! These thoughts from a Ligonier Ministries devotional might help us understand:

> When covenants were made in the ancient Near East, certain rites would accompany the agreement in order to signify what would happen if one or both parties failed to live up to their end of the pact. One common ritual involved dismembering animals and then laying the pieces in two rows side-by-side with a path between. The individuals making the covenant would then pass between the animals and invoke a curse upon themselves if they broke the agreement. In performing this rite both parties were in effect saying, "If I do not fulfill the terms of this covenant, may the destruction that befell these animals also be upon my head."[2]

Gulp!

The legally binding nature of a covenant was nothing to be messed with.

Now, here's what's astounding about what happened next: *only God walked through the row of sacrificed animals. Abram did not.*

To someone in the ancient world, it would have been unheard of for only the stronger of two parties to walk through the pieces of the animal sacrifice. But that's exactly what happened.

Once the bloody pieces were arranged, God caused Abram to fall asleep. Then God's presence moved between the pieces of sacrificed flesh.

This was significant.

God was stating the obvious: *Abram's not capable of keeping his end of the bargain.* And yet the God of the universe was declaring, "If this covenant is broken—and it will be—may I be as these bloodied sacrificed animals."

And eventually He was.

Jesus Christ would be broken and bloodied for us. When He died for you and for me, He was fulfilling the Abrahamic covenant and establishing a new one (Hebrews 9:15). His death was His faithful act to redeem us even though no human had ever lived up to the covenant agreements of the Old Testament.

Jesus' death on the cross both satisfied the law and protected the love.

Covenant Love

As I studied covenant, I learned that the Hebrew word *hesed* is a prominent piece of covenant language. It often shows up in our Old Testament translations as "love." But you can also find it translated as "goodness," "kindness," "faithfulness," "mercy," "devotion," "favor," and "steadfastness."

Why so many words? Because there is not an English or Greek word that adequately expresses God's covenant love for us.

Okay, here's where the hard thinking starts to pay off: God intended for marriage to portray *that* kind of love. Intimate. Unfailing. Sacrificial. Redemptive.

You can see this intention throughout the Bible. But the most succinct statement of the sacred purpose of marriage is found in the New Testament.

> **"Therefore, a man will leave his father and mother and hold fast to his wife, and the two will become one flesh." This mystery is profound, and I am saying that it refers to Christ and the church.**
> **—EPHESIANS 5:31–32**

Marriage should be characterized by unfailing love because it was meant to portray unfailing covenant love. And that kind of love possesses unique staying power. Why? Because it's focused on the needs of the other person, not personal happiness.

Am I saying you can't be happy in a covenant marriage? Of course not. I've often experienced tremendous joy and happiness in mine. But happiness is honestly beside the point. A covenant love is about something richer, deeper, more fulfilling and redemptive than just how we feel. And sometimes it takes a time of brokenness for us to understand the truth and the power of that kind of love.

The early love you experienced with your husband was wonderful (I hope). And it was important for establishing a foundation of connection between you. The excitement and tenderness you so often felt during your courtship, engagement, and even the early years of your marriage was a wonderful gift of love from God.

That's the easy part of painting the picture of the gospel, my friend.

But what happens when a marriage hits a broken place?

As I tried to find an answer for my own heart, I discovered a teaching presented by Tim and Kathy Keller. A single sentence flooded me with new hope:

> In a Christian marriage, each person
> gets to play the Jesus role.[3]
> —Kathy Keller

Kathy went on to say, "Together a husband and wife living out their roles of headship and submission can display the fullness of the glory of Christ and the gospel in a powerful way."[4] Her intention was to explain that women have the honor of displaying Christ's submission to the Father's plan (Philippians 2). And men have the responsibility to display the headship of Christ (Ephesians 5). When we do this well, both the husband and the wife "play the Jesus role."

Let me emphasize that doing this well is essential for a marriage to be an accurate portrayal of Christ's love. If only one individual determines to live according to covenant love, they are at incredible risk of being exploited by the other partner.[5] This is why wise counsel and mindful consideration are critical both before marriage and when a partnership hits a broken spot.

But when both husband and wife rise up to the expectations of covenant love, both "play the Jesus role."

What does that mean for you when your husband's sin has offended your covenant vows?

That's where what I call "after love" comes into play.

"After Love"

After love is driven by commitment to the covenant and overrides our emotions when they are put to the test by sin. Consider this amazing thought about the faithfulness of covenant love:

In a covenant, two people look at each other and say . . . "I will be what I should be whether you are being what you should be or not."[6]
—Tim Keller

After love is super easy for me when Bob is rising up—as he so often does—to be the Jesus part of our covenant love. I'm so grateful for his faithfulness and forgiveness when I . . .

> . . . confess sin from my past, or
>> . . . struggle with hormonal ebbs and flows, or
>>> . . . fall into a pattern of workaholism and
>>> ignore his desire to play.

Time and time again, Bob Gresh has been what he promised to be when I was not being what I promised I would be. This is a very significant piece of our marriage story.

You see, I had a secret when we got married. As I briefly mentioned in an earlier chapter, I was not a virgin on our wedding night. And the shame I carried from my previous sexual sin significantly impacted the intimacy of my relationship with Bob.

Several years into our marriage, this burden became too heavy to carry on my own. It took me three emotionally gut-wrenching hours to get a one-sentence confession out. But I finally mumbled an awkward sentence of truth, daring to believe that God's forgiveness—and Bob's covenant love—was big enough for the shame and sin I had carried for so long.

It was.

That night I began to experience the depth of God's redeeming love because my husband was what he promised he would be, even when I was not.

But I have gotten to play the Jesus part of the covenant picture too, of course. I have deliberately chosen what I promised I would be in those times when Bob has not been what he promised to be. When his heart has been heavy with shame and sin, I have done my very best to reach beyond my pain in order to protect the covenant we made on our wedding day.

And as I wrestled through my questions about whether my marriage relationship was a picture of the love of Christ, I came to an important conclusion.

the truth you need *Covenant love calls and equips us to be a picture of God's unfailing love—not in spite of sin and brokenness, but because of it.*

Jesus suffered and died out of love when we were unable to keep our end of the covenant law. Marriage becomes like our relationship with Christ when we rise up to protect the covenant when our partner cannot. And the love required of us when that happens is powerful and redemptive. It's not the fairy tale of two starstruck lovers, but the union between two great forgivers. And take it from me, it can bring you a lot of happiness. It's just a different kind of happy.

You just have to keep in mind where the love comes from in the first place.

Jesus First

Covenant love in marriage is so risky.

And difficult.

There's only one thing that will provide the power you need for the long haul, and that is being completely consumed with the unfailing love of Jesus Christ. Covenant love in marriage only works if you have first received the love relationship God initiates with you (1 John 4:19). And then love Him back with all your heart, soul, and strength (Mark 12:28–30).

First and foremost, you must experience the faithful love of Jesus Christ.

Have you?

I confess that this whole issue became muddy for me when Bob and I first entered into our marriage work. My heart wanted so badly for my husband to rescue me from my pain. But only Jesus could do that! I needed first and foremost to experience a deeper understanding of my Savior's love.

Friend, be sure you're not idolizing your marriage. Many Christians do. Codependency, abusive distortions of submission, and a domineering view of a husband's role result. These things are nurtured in a petri dish of untruth when we value the marriage more than we do our relationship with Jesus Christ.

Consider the fact that in heaven you won't be married at all—because being married in heaven doesn't make sense. Marriage, remember, is a *picture* of our intimacy with Christ. You won't need any representations of that intimacy when you are experiencing it face-to-face.

If I take you on a trip to Alaska, I may show you photographs of magnificent glaciers, powerful grizzly bears, and snow-capped mountains to whet your appetite. But once we get there, you won't need the pictures.

Marriage is important here on earth because it gives us a taste of the kind of relationship we will have with Jesus Christ once we see Him face-to-face. But take care that it does not become so preeminent in your heart that you forget what it's trying to teach you: to seek the love of God with all your heart, soul, and mind. Because that's what you were made to do. That's why you crave love in the first place. Because you were created for a relationship with a loving God.

Sister, God is inviting you to a deeper understanding of His love!

It's Time to Pray!

Sit quietly with Jesus today and soak in His love. After you have done that for a bit, pray these verses aloud:

My Beloved, help me to be like a bride adoring her loved one in my relationship with You. Let me hear Your voice. Come to me. Leap over the mountains of pain and trouble. Bound over the hills of long waiting and impatience. Come to me (Song of Solomon 2:8).

Jesus, thank You for enacting a new covenant with God the Father for us. I have accepted Your invitation to be part of Your relationship of love and law. Give me an understanding of the incredible inheritance You've promised to us who follow You. Oh Jesus, thank You for dying to release me from the guilt of the violations committed under the old covenant. You know I'm incapable of being faithful for this covenant agreement, but You promise to be faithful no matter what. I am undone by Your steadfast love (Hebrews 9:15; 1 Timothy 2:13).

Father God, I admit to You that I deeply desire to be loved. Right now it seems I'm feeling a deficit of love. Help me to be deeply satisfied with Your steadfast love and to compassionately love my husband out of it (Proverbs 19:22).

In the name of Jesus Christ,

Amen!

He has delivered us from the domain of darkness
and transferred us to the kingdom of his beloved Son,
in whom we have redemption, the forgiveness of sins.

—COLOSSIANS 1:13–14

As you work through this part of the book you might want to listen
to the *Happily Even After* limited-series podcast. Use this QR code
to find and listen to the pilot episode.

part three

Inviting God to Redeem the Story of Your Marriage

It's time to do the work of engaging with your husband and strengthening your marriage together. In this final part of the book I'd like to share seven truths to help you both welcome God's redeeming power into your covenant love.

Pain is not the problem. It's the gift.

—Pete Kuiper

chapter nine

Truth #1: Emotions Are Essential Ingredients of Intimacy

Above all else, guard your heart,
for everything you do flows from it.
—PROVERBS 4:23 NIV

After being apart for individual therapy, Bob and I were finally together again. The treatment program we'd first put our trust in turned out to be a disappointment, but we had no intention of quitting. I frantically made calls, and together we decided on Crossroads Counseling of the Rockies.

We were in for a thoroughly Christ-centered two-week therapy program. It included a course taught by our marriage counselor, whom I'd just met. Pete Kuiper stood at the front of our little classroom, a lanky, white-haired stranger. He had kind blue eyes and a disarming presence.

Pete already felt like a friend.

"All of us develop our own pain management skills," he began.

Hmm, I thought. *For the first time in a long time, I'm not feeling any pain.* My heart was locked up, safe and sound. As soon as I arrived here with Bob, it seemed to have gone numb.

How ironic that this entire lecture was an invitation to *feel*.

"Pain is God's alarm system," Pete explained. "It's telling you something is wrong. Pain is not the problem. It's the gift."[1]

None of us wants to feel the emotional pain when our husbands hurt us. But there are two things you need to know:

- Your emotional pain is a gift.
- Your emotional presence is the very medicine your husband's heart needs right now.

In other words, don't shut down.

Even though staying open can be really, really hard.

Consciously or unconsciously, you've developed strategies through the years to cope with your emotional pain. Your favored "pain meds" are as unique as you are, but they may include unhealthy options like these:

- **impulsive spending**
- **overeating or undereating**
- alcohol abuse
- illegal drugs or overuse of prescription drugs
- **oversleeping, sometimes with the aid of sleeping pills**
- **overachieving or overworking**
- **isolating from community**
- **routinely scrolling mindlessly through social media feeds**
- superficial or rote religious routines or rituals

- superficial happiness ("fake it till you make it")
- self-pity
- excessive anger
- appearance management
- sexually acting out
- being someone's "savior" (for the record, that's codependency)
- overcontrol of our environment or relationships
- **emotional numbness**
- **bitterness**

tell me your story

Circle any of the unhealthy pain-relief strategies listed above that you have employed in the past or may be utilizing even now. I have marked in bold the strategies I've used.

Everything on that list could fall into one of two categories: 1) uncontrolled, sinful behavior *or* 2) symptoms of emotional unwellness. Either way, they reveal something important:

You are being deceived.

Lies are Satan's primary tool to keep you and your husband in bondage to sin and pain (John 8:44). And he uses many different strategies to communicate his deception. The internet, streaming services, popular songs, societal input, and even our friends can be used to lead us from God's Truth. But sometimes the devil uses sources much closer to home, like family dysfunction, relational pain, and distorted childhood memories.

By their very nature, lies are sneaky and hard to detect. They easily slip into our belief systems, sometimes without our knowledge. And as we embrace them one by one, the destruction begins to take a toll.

Could that be where you and your husband are right now? Buried under no small amount of sin, emotional confusion, and pain—the forensic evidence that Satan has been at work.

When this happens we often mistake the pain as the problem.

In fact, it's a very big part of the solution.

the truth you need) *Truth #1: Emotions are essential ingredients of intimacy.*

Redeeming Your Emotions

Humans are complex beings. God made us with bodies (including our brains), souls, and spirits, all intimately entwined. As we have seen in earlier chapters, what happens in one influences the others. For instance, our brain chemistry can influence our feelings and behavior, and our feelings and behavior, in turn, influence our brain chemistry. The same is true of our beliefs, our emotions, and our behavior.

Think of your life as a tree. In fact, the Bible uses tree imagery to speak of the potential you have to be a life-giving, fruitful human being (Psalm 1:3, Isaiah 61:3). What people see above the surface—your behavior—results from what happens under the surface. And an important part of what is under the surface is your *belief system*.

When you have holy beliefs, your emotions are healthy and your behaviors are holy. This is God's goal for you.

When you have lies growing in your heart, however, your emotions are unhealthy and your behavior is sinful. This is Satan's goal for you.

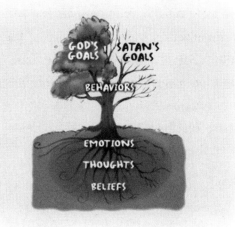

Pete Kuiper helped me begin to recognize important language the Bible often uses for our belief system. In his book *At the Crossroads*, Pete writes,

> The word the Bible most often uses when referring to the belief system is the heart. Rarely is it referring to the organ that pumps blood, but rather the deepest part of who you are as a human being. Jesus points out, "For a man's words depend on what fills his heart. A good man gives out good—from the goodness stored in his heart; a bad man gives out evil—from his store of evil" [Matthew 12:35].[2]

So how do we know what's going on under the surface, deep down in our hearts? God gave us emotions for this purpose.

Emotions communicate what's going on in your heart.

I like to think of emotions as the skin of your soul. Just as the epidermis of your body communicates messages of warning when you touch a hot pot, your emotions will warn you when your soul is in danger. And that's a very good thing.

The fact that emotions contain messages is very important. This is why I've already mentioned it a time or two. But it's also important to recognize that sometimes the lies we fall for and harbor in our hearts are *about* emotions. Satan wants us to believe these untruths because when we do, our God-given gift of receiving important messages from our souls cannot function.

What are these lies about emotions? Consider if you or your husband holds any of them in your heart:

- **Lie #1: Emotions don't matter. Just ignore them and they'll go away.** (They won't. Unless you respond to their message, they'll either resurface again and again or go underground and trigger all sorts of dysfunctional behavior.)
- **Lie #2: Emotions are dangerous and troublesome and need to be pushed down or hidden.** (Invisible or repressed emotions are more likely to drive sinful behavior and sabotage intimacy than emotions honestly recognized and shared.)
- **Lie #3: Emotions cannot be controlled.** (As my friend Nancy DeMoss Wolgemuth says, "The Enemy uses this lie to make us believe we have no choice but to be controlled by our emotions. While there's a sense in which we can't help the way we feel, the Truth is that we don't have to let our feelings run our lives."[3])

It's not hard to see where these lies come from. Many of them we learn in childhood. Others develop in reaction to hard or painful experience. Some are ideas we hold consciously, while others may fester under the surface of consciousness. But they all can create trouble for a marriage because they can cause us to shut down or turn off emotions.

Keep Your Heart Soft

Let's drill down on this now because when you're working on your marriage, you must not turn your emotions off. The Bible calls that "hardening your heart" and makes it clear that nothing good comes from it.

> **Whoever hardens his heart will fall into calamity.**
> **—PROVERBS 28:14**

You and your husband have had enough calamity. It's time to let God's Truth take you down a different path. And for that you must maintain a soft heart so you can read the message your emotional pain is communicating.

Keeping a soft heart also enables you to hear the Truth of God's Word. Check out what happened to the Israelites when they hardened their hearts.

> They made their hearts diamond-hard lest they should hear the law and the word that the LORD of hosts had sent by his Spirit.
> —Zechariah 7:12

Developing a hard heart leads to an inability to receive the Truth of God's Word. It disables your sensitivity to the Holy Spirit. It also short-circuits your ability to connect intimately with other people, even those closest to you (like your spouse).

So I beg you, let yourself *feel*. Even when it really hurts! If you're numb and not feeling very much at a given moment, ask God to help you recognize and listen to your emotions.

And no, I haven't always practiced what I'm preaching here. When Bob and I were working on our marriage, my emotions shut down almost completely. This eventually resulted in a sin produced by my hard heart: *bitterness.*

Pulling Up a Bitter Root

The dictionary defines bitterness this way:

Bitterness · "anger and disappointment at being treated unfairly; resentment."[4]

It's okay to feel angry over your husband's sin. In fact, it's probably inevitable. But bitterness results when you invite those angry feelings into your heart to set up residence—to become roots in your belief system.

Bitterness leads to destructive, sinful behavior. Many of the high-profile divorce cases that go to trial are saturated in this emotion. It is easy to see the bitterness at the root of the ugly behaviors that emerge in those proceedings. But most marriages experience it in the more common forms of unresolved anger, inability to grieve, and a lack of self-control. For me it looked like the silent treatment, emotional withdrawal, and the occasional furious outburst when the volcano of my anger built up.

I needed a transformation of my heart. I'll share how that happened in the next chapter. For now, I want you to know how it began.

One day I was listening to a podcast—I do not recall which one—when God's Spirit got out a heavenly chalkboard to teach me an important lesson. The host said bitterness includes the inability to be compassionate toward the person who is the object of your resentment.

Bingo! I immediately recognized what was happening with me.

I had run out of compassion for Bob.

Compassion · "an emotional response to empathy or sympathy [that] creates a desire to help."[5]

I was weary of the battle my husband faced with the enemy of his soul. I no longer had the inclination to understand his experience (sympathy) or to share his pain (empathy). And I definitely wasn't feeling inclined to help him.

You might be at this point too. Your husband has caused pain in your life. The instinct to pull away is evidence of your intelligent design. God programmed your emotions to keep your soul safe. If there is not some measure of pulling away from him when he hurts you, *you are not well.*

But you are also unwell if—after your husband begins to express repentance and breakthrough—you remain controlled by an emotion that has already completed its work of providing safety for your heart. God has also programmed you to have compassion for someone who is in spiritual bondage.

Don't let bitterness, numbness, and hardness of heart cause you to disengage from this spiritual battle! Confess those things to God and ask Him to help you recover your compassion and desire to help.

You may be thinking, "Dannah, why are you telling me this? I don't want to talk about my sin. I want to address my husband's!"

I know. That's precisely *why* I'm telling you.

Because the lies that you've believed about your emotions and your resulting behaviors—especially shutting down those emotions—run completely counter to the work of redeeming your husband's heart, healing your own wounded heart, and rebuilding your marriage.

And your emotional presence is one of the medicines your husband's sin-sick soul needs most to remedy the lies in *his* heart.

The Medicine Your Husband Needs

The behaviors of using pornography, preoccupation with sex, obsessive masturbation, visiting chat rooms, and other sinful escalations are go-to pain remedies for many men. And they, too, are rooted in lies. Your husband cannot walk in freedom—and your marriage cannot flourish—until the lies that have led to his spiritual bondage are ripped out and replaced with Truth, particularly the truth about emotions.

Psychologist Douglas Weiss makes this point vividly in his groundbreaking book, *Intimacy Anorexia*. He coined the term "intimacy anorexia" to describe "the active withholding of emotional, spiritual, and sexual intimacy."[6] (Sound familiar?) And he specifically tied sex addiction with this intimacy disorder:

> An intimacy anorexic who is a sex addict . . .
> cannot heal from intimacy anorexia unless
> the sex addiction is treated.[7]
> —Douglas Weiss

In other words, your husband has also experienced or is suffering from hardness of heart, which has caused him to shut down emotionally and have trouble experiencing true intimacy. And this hardness of heart is directly connected with his sin.

In Ephesians, Paul speaks of Gentiles who are trapped "in the futility of their minds." And what behaviors result?

> They are darkened in their understanding, alienated from the life of God because of the ignorance that is in them, **due to their hardness of heart**. They have become callous and **have given themselves up to sensuality**, greedy to practice every kind of impurity.
> —Ephesians 4:19

Hardheartedness is a highway to sexual sin.

What caused your husband's hardheartedness? According to Jay Stringer, many men—not all—who struggle with addiction have experienced one of five traumas as children:

- sexual abuse, either overt or subtle forms such as viewing porn with an older person or authority figure
- rigid and/or disengaged family systems
- parents who expected their child to fulfill the emotional role of partner (which is called enmeshment)
- abandonment or neglect
- a history of trauma (such as the death of a sibling or parent)[8]

Without someone to help him sort out the emotions of complex tragedy, your husband's heart may have become hard when he was just a little boy.

Of course, not everyone who uses pornography experienced significant trauma as a child. The catalyst for sin in our lives is as unique as each sinner. Sometimes it's just cultural norms or curiosity that lead to pornography use and other sexual sin. But after twenty years of counseling hurting hearts, I've observed that those who have trauma in their history usually have a harder time overcoming their sinful behavior. No matter how the problem began, however, there's room for compassion.

So let's get some compassion planted in your roots of belief.

Planting Compassion

One thing that helps my compassion is realizing how young many men were when *they first encountered pornography.*

It's hard to determine exactly when that is for most kids. But recent studies indicate that many children encounter it before their thirteenth birthday, with some children being as young as seven.[9] I was talking with a psychologist the other day who said she'd been working with two men who got their start when they were five and six. (I'm shaking my head in sadness as I type.)

Many of these initial encounters are prompted by simple curiosity, of course. But even then, childhood exposure can easily result in a lifetime of addiction, especially if it comes on top of trauma. Here's just an example of how it may happen.

A boy experiences a trauma—a distant mother, a workaholic father, abuse, neglect, bullying at school—and his heart begins to toughen up, desperate to not feel the pain. One day, he stumbles upon the poster of a celebrity in a swimsuit. It awakens an overwhelming mixture of pleasure. He buys the poster and hangs it in his bedroom.

In days that follow, when the boy closes the door and looks at the poster, he forgets the pain. That's because his brain produces a chemical called *dopamine*. You may remember reading about that earlier in the book. It's a neurotransmitter known as the "feel good" hormone.

It's nice to feel that way instead of sad. But that good feeling may well mark the pathway to devastation.

Because of the trauma in his family, no one notices the poster or why the boy may have it in his room. In other words, he has no one practicing intimacy with him. Before long he begins to wonder what that celebrity looks like underneath the spandex. He only has to type one word into a search engine to find the answer to his curiosity. Then bam—the glow of seduction illuminates his tiny little face.

The seed of addiction has begun to take root. And if nothing changes, it's likely to get worse.

Breaking the Sad Cycle

Most addictions involve external sources such as alcohol, nicotine, methadone, or even cake (if your addiction is sugar). As these *chemical addictions* progress, the user needs more of the chemical to maintain the level of dopamine output. And because "dopamine loves novelty,"[10] the user also seeks out new sources of stimulation.

This is largely true for *behavior addictions* such as gambling, shopping, and—yes—sexual addiction, including porn addiction. That means there's a significant risk of escalating behavior—to more graphic forms of porn and/or to acting out sexually by meeting people in hotels or hiring prostitutes.[11] (Read that last sentence again if you're thinking your husband's problem will just go away!)

Meanwhile, despite those periodic infusions of dopamine, your husband is probably feeling increasingly worse about himself and his addiction. Here are some thoughts that may run through his head: *No one loves me. I'm not lovable. I'm not worthy of my wife. I'm not a good enough man to be a father. I don't deserve this family. I do deserve to lose them. It would be better if I were dead.*

Deep down, a husband who uses sex as medicine feels his separation from God (Isaiah 59:2) and from his wife. His loneliness is a deep pain that he is hopeless to remedy on his own. But rather than press in to his need to feel closer to God and others, he self-medicates the discomfort with more sinful behavior. That makes him feel more shame and increases his need for more pain management. So the sad cycle goes.

He is terrified of intimacy—the very medicine he needs to overcome his sinful behavior. And no amount of white-knuckling to behave differently will ever work.

The lethal roots in his heart need to be ripped up!

Christian recording artist Jimmy Needham was only nine years old when a friend said, "Hey, there's a magazine buried under the rocks at the playground down the street. Let's go check it out."[12] That was the beginning of a decade of spiritual bondage to pornography.

For most of the next ten years Jimmy looked at pornography nearly every day.[13]

He did not begin to gain traction over his sinful desires until he started to pursue emotional intimacy. This required humility in front of other men.

"I was blessed with just a really great group of guys...." says Jimmy. "We were all believers, and we all were fighting for the same thing. One hundred percent of us were struggling with it.... **Having guys to fight alongside me who could pray for me, and I them, was a massive thing**. I don't think it was possible for me to find lasting freedom without doing that in the context of community."[14]

What happens in groups like that? Men get real. They tell their stories, cry tears of pain, use emotional language, and love each other like brothers.

The naked expression of emotions helps men discover the true medication for their pain: intimacy.

Jimmy also credits his wife, my friend and fellow author Kelly Needham, with opening his heart to God's grace. I am convinced that a man cannot fully recover from pornography without intimate friendship with men. And if he is married, he needs an emotional connection with his wife.

Learning to Feel Again

When I realized that my bitterness was at cross purposes to our marriage's redemption, I began to ask God to soften my heart toward Bob and to give me compassion for him. I knew it would take no small application of God's grace to bring this change to my angry heart. I also knew the process would probably be excruciating. But I gave the Lord permission to crush me with the emotions I needed to feel so I could walk with Bob in intimacy.

About that time, I found a photograph of my husband. He was maybe three years old when it was taken, but I recognized him easily because he was wearing a red shirt. My man loves wearing red shirts and sports one almost every day. I put that photograph by my bed.

For many months, I looked at that photo and prayed, "Lord, use me as a tool of your redemption. Give me compassion for the pain in that little boy's heart."

God answered that prayer. Not right away, but over time I began to cry tears that were different. They were not expressions of my broken heart, but intercessory petitions for his.

Inviting God to soften your heart and let you feel both pain and compassion is an essential ingredient of intimacy.

You might even go looking for an old picture—one of the boy who fought a battle alone. Keep it by your bed and ask the Lord to plant compassion in the roots of your heart. It's a medicine your husband's heart needs.

And you need it too!

As you work through this part of the book you might want to listen to the *Happily Even After* limited-series podcast. Use this QR code to find and listen in to the one that corresponds to this chapter.

Growing in Intimacy:
Talk with Your Husband about **Emotions**

Ha! I know. He's gonna love this, right? Well, it's really an essential conversation. Emotions, remember, are the skin of our souls. They protect us, but only if we respond to their messages with the Truth of God's Word. This requires taking an honest inventory of how we feel and transparently sharing with others who can help us read the message and respond appropriately. There is no person more important to explore emotions with than your spouse.

As we have seen, most men who experience sexual addiction are suffering from an intimacy disorder. They are terrified of emotional connection, but that is precisely what they need.

Take some time to talk through Truth #1 together:

Emotions are essential ingredients of intimacy.

1. When you were a child, were you encouraged to stuff down your emotions or to maturely express them? Tell a story that illustrates your answer.

2. One way you can grow in your ability to be emotionally healthy is to practice emotional check-ins. Take time to stop what you are doing and assess how you feel. Communicate it to your spouse. An important part of this exercise is not to interrupt the other person or try to change how they feel. Just listen. Let's try it now. Select one emotion from the six basic emotions below that best expresses how you feel right now. Communicate why you feel that way.

sadness	**happiness**
fear	**anger**
surprise	**disgust**

3. What message do you think this emotion is trying to communicate to you about what's going on in the roots of your belief system?

4. How do you think God wants you to respond to it? And what can your spouse do to help you?

5. Pray together. Ask God to keep your hearts soft toward one another as you work through your emotions about your current struggle.

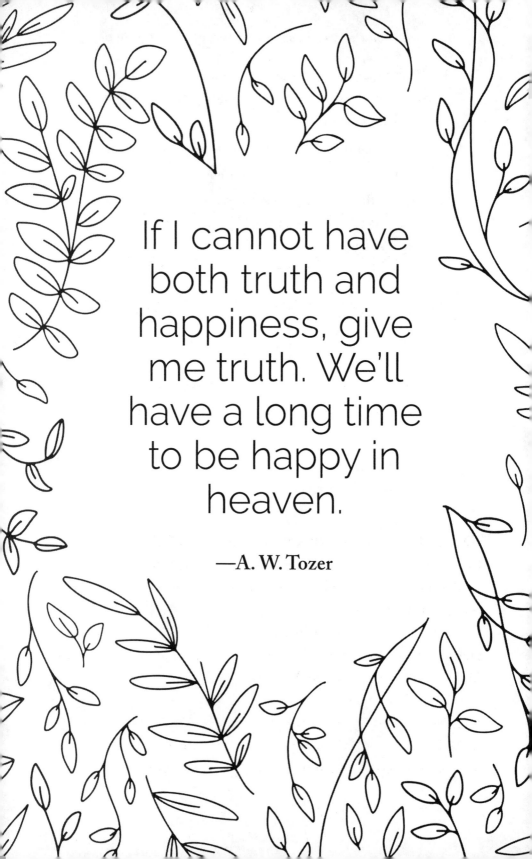

If I cannot have
both truth and
happiness, give
me truth. We'll
have a long time
to be happy in
heaven.

—A. W. Tozer

chapter ten

Truth #2: Honest Confession Is the Beginning of Healing

Therefore, confess your sins to one another and pray for one another, that you may be healed. The prayer of a righteous person has great power and it is working.

—JAMES 5:16

"Dannah, you're emotionally divorced," challenged Pete Kuiper, my wise counselor who had become a dear friend.

Bob and I had been to Colorado for several intensives, then Pete had begun counseling us by phone. Today I was getting a private session.

Divorce was not a word that Bob and I used—ever. And I was proud of that. My mind raced to find a defense, but I didn't have one. My heart was shut down, and I knew it.

For nearly two months, I'd been sleeping in the extra bedroom. It started because my back injury had flared up. My doctor had prescribed sleeping on the floor, but an extra-firm mattress—even if it felt like concrete—seemed to give my bones enough support.

My back had been feeling better for some time now. But my heart had been feeling . . . well, not much. And part of me liked it. I liked not hurting. Physical pain had become an excuse to keep my distance from Bob so I could avoid the emotional pain.

I was self-medicating with numbness again.

Under Pete's supervision, Bob had provided full disclosure on every secret and sin that his heart had known. Pete had been compassionate when I told them both, "I'm not ready to forgive."

Our first intensive had ended in an emotional stalemate. Bob and I had driven away in silent sadness.

But now Pete was holding my feet to the fire with a complete awareness of how hot it was.

"You're at a crossroads," he said.

Then Pete added something that shocked me into silence: "Dannah, you need to decide if you'll let Jesus do CPR to your heart. Because if you don't let Him, your marriage story is over. Even if there's not a piece of paper to prove it."

It was a cataclysmic moment of truth.

Complete honesty is an integral part of redeeming a marriage. But I won't lie. Full disclosure is going to hurt.

A lot.

In fact, one reason I'd reached that point of emotional divorce was that our work with Pete included hearing the full confession of Bob's sins. That's something that you've probably experienced or will need to in the future. The counseling world calls it *disclosure.*

Disclosure · "a mutual, planned, facilitated event where your husband reads to you a document he has prepared that contains the whole truth regarding his sexual sin."[1]

As helpful as this step of healing is in the long run, it's one of the most wounding experiences you'll ever have in your entire life. Many women tell me they do not want to hear these details. They believe this lie: *hearing the truth will destroy me.*

That's simply not true.

Truth does not destroy us. It sets us free (John 8:31–32). Honest confession is the medium that positions us to be redeemed by God. And it is appropriate that confession includes those who have been sinned against. First John reads like this:

> If we say we have fellowship with him while we walk in darkness, we lie and do not practice the truth. But if we walk in the light, as he is in the light, we have fellowship with one another, and the blood of Jesus his Son cleanses us from all sin. If we say we have no sin, we deceive ourselves, and the truth is not in us. If we confess our sins, he is faithful and just to forgive us our sins and to cleanse us from all unrighteousness.
> —1 John 1:6–9

When you confess sin to another believer and hear another's confession, you are inviting the Savior into your circumstance, allowing Him to use Truth to set you free from your spiritual bondage. This is the antivenom for the sting of Satan's lies. It feels destructive, but I encourage you to administer this medicine bravely, trusting God's ability to heal you both.

| **the truth you need** | 〔 *Truth #2: Honest confession is the beginning of healing.* |

Because disclosure can be so painful, I highly recommend that you lean into this hard task with the help of your clinically informed, biblically grounded support team. But let's see if I can help prepare your mind and heart.

In Full Disclosure

During his confession your husband will be asked to answer questions like these:

- What was your sexual history prior to marriage?
- What types of pornography have you viewed? Where? On which devices? How often?
- Did your sexual sin ever escalate beyond pornography?
- Have there been any forms of acting out with other individuals? What forms? When did this occur? How often?
- If there are sex partners, how many? Who (if they are people that you know)? When did you last have contact with any of these partners?
- Do you have any sexually transmitted diseases? Have you been tested?

I told you it would be painful.

Thankfully, my husband was able to answer "no" to a bunch of these questions. But some of his answers still crucified me emotionally.

Do you really need to go through *that*? Yes and no. Let's talk about what healthy confession looks like.

You need to hear categorically *everything he has done, because it is the door to emotional intimacy.*

Your husband has spent months, years, or decades living a double life. He's put time and energy into creating an image of himself that is not truthful because his personal pain involves lies that tell him he is unlovable and unworthy. If he can share his deepest secrets and still be loved and accepted, he has a greater chance to experience sustained victory over his addiction to pornography or other sexual strongholds. Why? Because you're helping him to rip up the roots of lies he has believed about himself.

Some men try to wriggle around this important step in couple's work by confessing their sin to other men instead of their wives. Unfortunately, these individuals often continue escalating, eventually participating in even more perverse sin.

Debbie Laaser wishes her husband had disclosed his sin to *her* sooner.

Mark, who struggled with masturbation and pornography, escalated to crossing the flesh line early in their marriage. He confessed his sin to a pastoral counselor, who told him not to mention it to Deb because "it will hurt her." And then his adviser told him simply, "Don't ever do it again."[2]

Unfortunately, the pastor's unhelpful advice robbed Mark of the opportunity to live in truth with Debbie and for both to get help. He got in the way of Mark going after the root cause of his behaviors and, in doing so, allowed Mark's addiction to grow and worsen. And it did for ten more years until there was discovery again.

Debbie says, "The next ten years might have been very different if the facts had been out and the process of forgiving and healing could have begun."[3]

Instead, there was a vicious secret separating the pair. Their marriage was robbed of the opportunity to do the hard work of emotional intimacy. And without that, those struggling with sex addiction and their spouses cannot recover.

Your husband's addiction will escalate without disclosure.

I told you this in the last chapter when I explained that an addiction to dopamine through sexual outlets requires "more" and "novel" to sustain the "feel good" response to the hormone. Here's what the progression may look like in a man's life:

1. **Early exposure**, often the result of curiosity, draws the child or young man in. The resulting release of dopamine and other "feel good" chemicals provide comfort and excitement, luring him to try it again.
2. **Addiction** develops as curiosity turns into physiological dependency. Porn is needed for arousal, and the man depends on the "feel good" chemicals for physical and emotional satisfaction.
3. **Desensitization** occurs when the standard sexual "fix"— whether "normal" pornography or sex in a relationship— no longer provides the same pleasure or excitement. This reduced gratification fuels the desire for greater stimulation.
4. **Escalation** means the man seeks novel ways to get his dopamine fix. He may seek out more transgressive and objectifying pornography or turn to chat rooms, sexting, inappropriate social media conversations, or cybersex. Sex in the marriage becomes even less frequent and may

become more transactional and demanding rather than intimate and fulfilling.

5. **Acting out sexually** is the next stage and could include meeting people in hotels, hiring prostitutes, or having affairs.[4]

tell me your story

How far has your husband escalated in his sinful behavior? In the list of progressive behaviors, draw a line under the level where you think he is functioning.

I know that's a very hard list to consider. I'm sorry. But I need you to know that you must courageously face things that other women—like me—have survived! Many of our marriages are stronger because of it. (In fact, I have good news about Mark and Debbie Laaser, which I'll share in a future chapter!)

Hearing your husband's confession will be painful, but it is actually a very positive step. A man who is willing to confess his sin to you is a man who is willing to be made well.

That does not mean that Satan won't use this process to drive you mad. His tool: your own questions.

Crushing Questions

Inevitably disclosure begins to produce questions in your mind. Should you ask them? That depends on your husband's sin, your personality, and other factors.

I know; you wanted a clearer answer. But I can't give you that.

I will tell you that it's critical to have a counselor support you in figuring out what is healthiest for you as an individual and as a couple. I have seen many marriages damaged by too much information.

As you know from a previous chapter, I have confessed to Bob that I was sexually active with one guy before we were married. But that's all he knows. We've agreed that the details would not help either of us.

When Bob confessed his sin to me, he told me that he would answer any questions I had. My counselor advised me to ask myself, "Is the answer to this question going to help me heal?" If I sensed that it would not, I had to execute self-control. But if I sensed that the answer was an important part of our process, I would ask the question that was crushing me. Bob never failed to answer my questions, but he was careful not to be too detailed in his answers. That worked for us.

Some women, especially those whose husbands have had an affair, discover that knowing the details is more important to them. One woman told me, "I don't want the other woman knowing something about him that I do not." Her marriage is, in fact, thriving today.

You'll need some guidance to determine what works for you and your marriage. Tell your counselor about your curiosities and let him or her help you. That's what you pay them to do.

Your Most Powerful Tool

There may be times when you feel you are clinging to your last shred of sanity during this process. Don't forget, you and I have a tool that the world's recovery programs could not possibly understand. In fact, they think it foolish. They have only their natural brains to work with when facing the daunting work of confession and forgiveness. Believing sister, you have something more powerful.

You have the mind of Christ given to you through the Spirit of God!

When the pictures your husband has planted in your head attempt to consume your thoughts, you can invite the Holy Spirit to give you wisdom from God. The way you think about those things can be renewed (1 Corinthians 2:5–16; Romans 12:2).

I had to remind myself of this continually: *I have the mind of Christ!* And I prayed things like this: "Lord, my mind has been devastated by sin. Please redeem it. Open the eyes of my heart to know the hope to which I have been called" (Ephesians 1:18).

Speaking of prayer, this is a good time to remind you that prayer is your weapon! If I had it to do over again, I would approach disclosure day with prayer and fasting. And here's what I would pray, based on Ephesians 1:18–22:

> Lord, may our hearts be flooded with light so we can understand the confident hope we have in Jesus Christ. As Your son and daughter, we have a rich and glorious inheritance of love. I pray that You will give us new understanding of the incredible greatness of God's power for us who believe in Jesus Christ. That same power which raised Christ from the dead and seated Him in a place of honor at God's right hand can redeem this broken marriage, my broken heart, and my husband's broken intimacy. You are far above any rule or power or authority or anything else in this world. I feel a tad over my head. Help me to remember **it is still under Your feet!**

May you pray this and believe that the entire disclosure process is under the feet of Jesus, our redeeming Savior.

And for the moments when you get it wrong—for those times when you walk in fear or bitterness—remember that the same grace your husband needs is still life and breath to your own soul.

My Confession

As you know, an individual therapy appointment revealed that I was not walking in forgiveness. We'll cover that topic soon. For now, know that it was long overdue in the Gresh house because I had fallen into a pit of bitterness.

Pete asked me if I knew what Jesus said about divorce? My thoughts immediately went to adultery, but Pete said that wasn't exactly right. Jesus said, "Because of your hardness of heart Moses allowed you to divorce" (Matthew 19:8). The root that produces the behavior of divorce is ultimately hardness of our hearts. It is because men and women try to control behaviors rather than nurturing roots of Truth that they eventually fall prey to the sadness of divorce.

God wanted to address the root of bitterness which was growing in my heart. My heart was often like cold, hard granite.

Is yours?

After I talked on the phone with Pete, I went into my office and cuddled up with a cozy blanket and a cup of tea. I reached for my Bible.

"Jesus, is our story over?" I prayed.

Then, I opened my Bible and read 1 Peter. Wow! What a follow-up. God's Spirit was tag-teaming it with my counselor that day. Let me show you what I read. Pay special attention to the italicized words.

> *The end of all things is at hand; therefore be self-con-trolled and sober-minded for the sake of your prayers. Above all, keep loving one another earnestly, since love covers a multitude of sins.* **Show hospitality to one another without grumbling. As each has received a gift, use it to serve one another, as good stewards of God's varied grace: whoever speaks, as one who speaks oracles of God;** *whoever serves, as one who serves by the strength that God supplies*—**in order that in everything God may be glorified through Jesus Christ. To him belong glory and dominion forever and ever. Amen.**
> —1 PETER 4:7–11

This treasure in God's Word moved me. Deeply. It was a turning point for me in a way that's difficult to describe. But let me try because there's sweetness here for your heart.

These words are from a letter Peter wrote to suffering Christians. They were in exile because of their faith. This entire book of the Bible is about how to respond to and live through suffering. The recipients of the letter could be described as crushed, overwhelmed, devastated, torn, and broken.

Does that sound like you? Then lean in.

Now, the recipients of Peter's letter were facing trials as a direct result of persecution for resolutely refusing to deny the name of Jesus Christ. But early in the book Peter says his writing is for people with *various* kinds of suffering (1 Peter 1:6), not just the Christian persecution kind. I think this safely includes the married kind.

Now, some scholars think "the end of all things" referred to in 1 Peter 4 is talking about the end of the world, making them kinda gloomy words. Others think of this as finish-line encouragement language, making them "you can do it" words! Either way, Peter is promising that suffering will come to an end. (I like that, don't you?)

Until then, he prescribes self-control and sobriety *"for the sake of your prayers."*

Have you been praying

> ... for your husband's heart to return to yours? And to Jesus?
> ... for him to step up and lead in your relationship?
> ... for your heart to awaken or heal?
> ... for his computer and phone to blow up into a thousand pieces so he can never look at porn again?

Been there. Done that.

For the sake of *those* prayers, you've got to figure out what it means to be self-controlled and sober-minded! I'm pretty sure a self-controlled, sober-minded woman doesn't self-medicate her pain. She chooses to take it to the Lord rather than become drunk on her drug of choice, be it work or appearance management or vodka.

But that's not where I really want to land today. It's just a bonus thought.

Let me tell you what worked like a defibrillator to my emotionally dead heart when I read this passage. It was that next thing in the verse that brought life to my spirit. The thing about love covering a "multitude of sins."

Bob had disclosed to me a multitude of sins. It was as if these verses were telling me that the answer to my prayers was to simply love him.

Ugh. That seemed so unfair!

And yet in my heart I could sense God's Spirit saying, *Dannah, I need you to feel. I need you to love. That's your part in this sin battle Bob's facing.*

I didn't want to do my part of the battle. I wanted Bob to have eyes for me alone. I needed him to chase me around the bedroom and grit his teeth with desire like he once had. I craved those heart-stopping love letters he used to write. And the last thing in the world I wanted was to *feel* the ugly reality of what our marriage had become.

So I had chosen numbness. And numbness is the opposite of what God instructs.

> Above all, keep loving one another earnestly,
> because love covers a multitude of sins.
> **−1 Peter 4:8**

Keep loving.

Earnestly.

It isn't fair, but it is true.

Love covers sin. Not just a few sins, but a multitude. Has your husband sinned a whole "multitude" against you? Love can cover it.

When I realized I was emotionally divorced, I invited my Savior to do what He has done over and over again: rescue me. He awakened my heart with His love. You see, we're just about to get to the part of that 1 Peter passage that really resuscitated me.

This passage contains some good news about loving someone who has broken your heart: *you don't have to rely on your own ability to love them.* You'll need "the strength that God supplies." Without it you've got little hope of pulling off this kind of sin-covering love. (I guess it's a good thing that you've been strengthening yourself in the Lord.)

Frankly, I threw that Truth right back at Jesus in prayer: "Lord, I'll need a whole lot of Your strength if I'm going to do this. My supply is very low. Fill me with Your love."

And He did.

I realize that might sound simplistic! But I cannot explain to you the night-and-day difference of brokenhearted Dannah before

1 Peter 4:7–11 and truth-empowered Dannah after. I became happy. No, wait—it wasn't happiness.

I experienced joy!

Because my marriage still needed a lot of work, and my circumstances had not changed, but my heart had. It was opened to Bob in a way that I don't think it had ever been opened before. I was all in. No matter what. And I didn't have expectations for Bob to rescue me. I recognized fully that only Jesus could do that.

I came to Bob that evening and made my own confession.

I told him that I had given up. Told him I was sorry that I'd allowed emotional divorce to slip into the picture and that my hard heart was a dangerous, sinful mess! Told him I was committed to loving him well even though he was making it difficult at the moment. I even confessed that I didn't know how to love him, but that I was choosing to do so and trusting God's Spirit to teach me.

I slipped quietly into bed that night. Next to Bob.

There was no make-up sex, and I won't remember it as a fun night, but I honor it as the night my heart changed direction. I decided to keep it soft. And I really, truly loved Bob Gresh that night as I slipped off into *peaceful* sleep.

Honest confession is a starting place for healing and intimacy to grow in your marriage. This means you'll need to hear your husband's confession.

But don't be surprised if he ends up hearing one from you too!

As you work through this part of the book you might want to listen to the *Happily Even After* limited-series podcast. Use this QR code to find and listen in to the one that corresponds to this chapter.

Growing in Intimacy:
Talk with Your Husband about **Confession**

The questions you will discuss today are important, but I recommend strongly that you don't talk much beyond them without the help of a biblically based, clinically informed Christian therapist or someone else to guide the process of disclosure. You also both need your own people—accountability group or friends—who will help you carry the heavy weight of this hard work in the days following confession. But you can begin discussing when and where it will happen. As you discuss today's questions, keep in mind that each of you needs to answer the questions, not just your husband.

Begin by talking through Truth #2 together:

Honest confession is the beginning of healing.

1. Have you ever told anyone else the darkest sin you've ever committed? Or do you have secrets that weigh heavily on your heart that no one else knows? If the answer is yes, who can you talk to about this battle with sin so that you have a friend or friends who are entering into authentic community with you?

2. In the future, would you be willing to give your partner full disclosure about the secrets you carry? Using the six core emotions, how does providing full disclosure make you feel?

sadness	**happiness**
fear	**anger**
surprise	**disgust**

3. What steps can you take to move toward full disclosure with each other? When will you do it?

4. Pray together. Ask the Lord to protect the process of being honest and confessing sin to one another.

Note: If in the course of this conversation your husband says he is unwilling to proceed with disclosure, he is likely resisting the work of redemption. Talk to your counselor or advisers about how you should respond.

Boundaries
are good.
They help
us enjoy life.

chapter eleven

Truth #3: Boundaries Can Bring Holiness and Health to Your Life

Speaking the truth in love, we are to grow up in every way into him who is the head, into Christ.

—EPHESIANS 4:15

I didn't like it when I first began to feel it.

Unsure of what to call it, I grabbed my journal and drew a picture of what I was feeling.

Little Bob and Dannah stick figures filled opposite sides of the page. Funny, I seemed to be holding my heart at a distance.

I showed it to Tippy and described what I thought was going on with me. She told me it sounded like the beginning of *healthy detachment*.

"Please tell me that's a good thing," I said. Her answer echoed in my heart:

**"Detaching can be a scary place.
But it can be a holy place."**

How could it be healthy for me to be detached from Bob?

Well, I was getting my feet under me and gaining the capacity to respond to him objectively and honestly rather than spinning out emotionally. I was coming to terms with what I could accept in our lives together and what I could not tolerate. Most importantly, I was finally learning what I was responsible for, what Bob needed to do for himself, and what only God could do.

It was all part of learning to set appropriate *boundaries.*

Years ago, a social experiment was conducted with two groups of children. One group was directed to a playground with no fence, the other to one with a fence. The researchers discovered that those in the group without the fence explored less territory of the playground, while those who had the safety of a fence played freely in all parts of the playground.[1]

Boundaries can be a good thing. They protect us and free us to enjoy life. And this is just as true for broken marriages as it is for kids on a playground.

From the beginning, God has taken care to set up healthy boundaries for His children. In fact, a boundary was one of the first things He communicated to human beings. He told Adam and Eve, "Of the tree of the knowledge of good and evil you shall not eat, for in the day that you eat of it you shall surely die" (Genesis 2:17).

God intended this boundary—and others He later established—for the health and holiness of His beloved creation. Scriptural rules and precepts like the Ten Commandments are the God-given fences around this playground we call earth.

Your husband has been playing outside the fence.

And you can lovingly invite him back inside by establishing and protecting special boundaries.

Boundary in marriage • "a limit we set that protects the sacredness of our marriage."[2]

Boundary Disputes

The concept of setting boundaries in marriage can be controversial among Christians. Many women have believed the lie that setting boundaries is a worldly concept. Some believe they're not supposed to make anything off limits to their husbands.

Others discount the value of boundaries because they've seen them terribly misused. For example, my friend and her husband used to hang out with a couple whose marriage was troubled. The wife was always weaponizing sex to get what she wanted. In front of other people, she would threaten that he wasn't going to "get any" if he didn't observe her arbitrary boundaries. (Their marriage did not make it.)

At the opposite end of the spectrum, I've met women who seem to have completely lost their voices in their marriages. The experience of being constantly deceived and gaslit[3] by their husbands has rendered them unable to stand up for themselves.

These women were often in relationships with men who had become programmed by the porn they watched to be selfish and transgressive. Research has confirmed that pornography changes the way its users view sex. Instead of a loving act of giving of oneself to another, they begin to think of sex as an act of violence and greed. Some studies suggest that as many as 90 percent of pornography videos are physically transgressive. And at least one study indicated that nearly 50 percent of pornographic scenes analyzed contain verbal aggression, primarily in the form of name calling. Women are bearing the brunt of this trend as it bleeds into their marriage beds.[4]

Many women have come to me asking if they can say no to something their husband wants to do in the bedroom—anal sex, for instance.

Others are experiencing requests to fulfill the unusual fetishes of husbands who clearly need counseling. These women have endured all manner of abusive sexual appetites.

This was not *my* experience at all. Bob has always been a kind and safe lover. So I was surprised when women came to me seeking advice about what to do when their husbands began being abusive in the bedroom.

Would you tell these women that they should submit to abuse that feeds their husband's appetite for porn and other sexual transgressions? I did not.

I told them they had every right to say no to anything that made them feel uncomfortable, and I reminded them that a loving husband would honor that boundary. For those whose husbands were unduly discontent with such refusal, I suggested they seek professional help for their marriage immediately.

My advice to these women was partly rooted in logic and partly in compassion. But I also believe the Bible lays down a pattern of mutual consent when it comes to sex and marriage (more on this later). A holistic reading of Scripture characterizes the act of marriage as tender and compassionate—a giving of your whole self.

So in light of distortions and misunderstandings, let's try to redeem our understanding of healthy boundaries in a marriage broken by sexual sin.

Redeeming Our Understanding of Boundaries

The Bible communicates some of the basics for healthy marriage boundaries:

- **Covenant love.** Marriage is created by God as a lifelong, binding covenant between one man and one woman (Ephesians 5:31–32).

- **Honesty.** Trust and respect are critical ingredients in covenant relationships. Honesty is the boundary that protects them (Colossians 3:9; Proverbs 31:11).
- **Faithfulness.** The marriage bed is meant to be undefiled (Hebrews 13:4). There should not be even a hint of sexual sin among us (Ephesians 5:3). The relationship should reflect whole life, mind, and soul devotion (Matthew 19:6).
- **Humility.** Appropriate male leadership assumes a humble position—a husband laying his life down, reflecting the sacrificial nature of Christ's love. When a wife responds humbly and appropriately to her husband's leadership, she reflects the noble submission of Christ to do the will of His Father (Ephesians 5:22–33; 1 Corinthians 11:3).
- **Self-control.** Husbands and wives do fight, but they learn to communicate their disagreements and concerns mindfully to one another with the leading of the Holy Spirit (Galatians 5:16–26).
- **Safety.** A husband should protect and care for his wife (Ephesians 5:25–29). A wife's response to this is to help her husband in such a way that his heart trusts her completely (Proverbs 31:11).
- **Mutual consent.** Covenant love presupposes a love that cares about the other person's needs. This results in a mutual submission to those needs (Ephesians 5:21). This applies to what happens in the bedroom. The natural behavior of a married couple is to freely give their bodies to one another. But Scripture establishes the freedom to mutually abstain for an agreed-upon period of time dedicated to prayer (1 Corinthians 7:5).
- **Forgiveness.** Our lack of forgiveness toward others—including our husbands—disrupts the flow of God's

forgiveness toward our own hearts (Colossians 3:13; Matthew 6:14–15).

tell me your story

Circle any of the biblical boundaries listed on pages 170–72 that are currently being crossed or disregarded in your marriage.

If your husband is betraying your marriage vows and violating the boundaries that characterize a healthy biblical marriage, you need to confront his sin. If you keep silent, you are more than likely participating in the demise of your covenant. I invite you to hold firm regarding God's boundaries and to consider establishing your own boundaries that are unique to your needs.

The Purpose of Boundaries

The reason you follow biblical boundaries is to set a marriage apart as holy and to ensure relational health. But the purpose of establishing special boundaries when a marriage is in trouble is to save it.

Which brings us to another truth:

the truth you need *Truth #3: Boundaries can bring holiness and health to your life.*

Several months after Elaine Daugherty married the man of her dreams, he came to her with a department-store magazine in his hand. Jonathan told her he had masturbated while he looked at the pictures of women in the magazine. Elaine was devastated but told herself it could have been worse. She was glad he was "so godly to have confessed his sins without being caught."

Her next thought was that she needed to present herself more attractively. (Been there? Done that?)

Unfortunately, the magazine was just the tip of the iceberg. Jonathan's appetite had already escalated not only to online porn but far beyond. He began to use chat rooms to meet women online, visited strip clubs, and even hired prostitutes. Elaine told me, "Every night I prayed that I would die in my sleep because it hurt so badly."

After four years of this, when Elaine learned that Jonathan had actually met a woman at a hotel for sex, she came to the end of her patience. That night she packed her bags and left. She didn't realize it at the time, but in leaving she was establishing a boundary—a therapeutic separation—that ultimately brought Jonathan to his senses.

That was the beginning of the end of Jonathan's thirteen-year battle with sexual addiction.

Drawing a line in the sand—a special boundary—saved Jonathan and Elaine Daugherty's marriage.

Sometimes the boundary of a therapeutic separation can be healthy and holy. If you think you may benefit from one, I encourage you to seek counsel. You'll need support doing what you need to do and wisdom to know when it's time to come back together.

But separation isn't the only kind of special boundaries that can save a marriage. If your husband has been straying outside the fence of biblical marriage, he needs the body of Christ, including you, to confront his sin. Confession to Jesus brings us forgiveness, but the pattern in Scripture is that accountability and confession to one another is how we displace sinful habits, patterns, and strongholds—including sexual sin and sex addiction.

Setting special boundaries in a troubled marriage can be an important part of that process.

Practice Makes . . . Progress

When I first heard of the concept of boundaries in marriage, I was a skeptic. Perhaps you are too. The reason could be that you, like me, believe in the *oneness* of a Christian marriage and you want to preserve it. Why would I want to set down boundaries to keep us apart?

Okay, let's start with that. You and your husband are *one*. Hold that thought.

In the Sermon on the Mount, Jesus told His followers how to live in many areas of life. One of the topics He included was lust. He took the standards of holiness that His contemporaries embraced to a whole new level. They considered adultery a zero-tolerance zone. But Jesus said that simply looking at a woman and thinking lustful thoughts was actually crossing the line.

And then He said this:

> "If your right eye causes you to sin, tear it out and throw it away. For it is better that you lose one of your members than that your whole body be thrown into hell."
> **—Matthew 5:29**

Talk about boundaries!

Now this statement was clearly hyperbole. If it were possible to stop sin by plucking out eyes, there would be a lot of blind men and women in church. The point Jesus was making is that we must be willing to go to drastic measures to protect holiness.

And what is the purpose of going to such extremes? *To save a sinner from hell.* Your husband's fascination with unholy sex is nothing short of a demonic distortion of God's gift of intimacy from the pit of hell.

When I considered this, I wondered if my covenant relationship with my husband compelled me to take what felt like drastic measures to eliminate lust from our lives. From our oneness.

For me the answer was yes. That's when I decided to try implementing boundaries in our particular situation. I read many books about how to do it, filtered out what advice seemed like folly, and picked what seemed applicable for me. I then wrote a one-page document, printed it out, and presented it to Bob.

He consented.

And suddenly the battle shifted—dramatically.

I'm not sure if this is as true for Bob as it was for me. My boundaries weren't about changing him really. Only God could do that. But they did provide us with a helpful tool for communicating expectations. And that felt really good.

Now, I did not practice the art of establishing boundaries well at first. But as I learned and Bob leaned in, we finally began to make progress in the battle to overcome his sin.

I have come to think that boundaries in this kind of situation are most effective when the wife has someone help deciding upon them and implementing them. This helps avoid the temptation to use boundaries for retribution and gives the husband the added support of another godly influence. (My husband has two godly men who ask him hard questions and enforce boundaries on behalf of me and our marriage covenant. I love them dearly!)

Fence Building 101

To establish a boundary regarding your husband's sexual sin, you use observable data to draw a line that cannot be crossed without consequences. You then communicate it objectively to your husband, perhaps with the help of your marriage counselor or a trusted godly influence in your husband's life.

Here's an example of how that might work.

1. **Receive data.** Say you have discovered pornography on your husband's phone. You know that pornography is dangerous for your marriage and his brain.

2. **Pray and fast.** I believe it is critical for a Christian wife to spend extended time with the Lord as a preparation. You ask God to bring your husband to repentance and to empower your influence to win your husband back to Truth.

3. **Decide on a boundary.** What cannot be tolerated— biblically and for you personally? Though you are painfully aware that you are a sinner, too, you are aware that sexual sin is distinct in its impact. You will not look the other way.

4. **Determine a consequence.** For instance, if your husband does not join a biblically based and clinically informed support group within the next week, he needs to move to the guest bedroom. (For the record, during the years we had kids in our house, this would have been the sofa in the basement!)

5. **Communicate your boundary and consequence clearly and objectively to your husband.** "I love you and our marriage too much to let us be destroyed by pornography. If you do not join a support group within the next week, I would like you to move to the guest bedroom until you have a plan to overcome your sin."

6. **Enforce the boundary.** You gotta mean it when you
say it, my friend. If your husband does not do what you
have requested, you need to ask him to move out of your
bedroom or whatever the agreed-upon consequences may
be. If he won't comply, then *you* need to move out of the
bedroom or do something else that keeps the consequence
in place. He has to feel the truth that sin separates us from
God and each other. In setting the boundary, you're simply
helping a man whose thinking has become impaired to
remember that truth.

Let me urge you to communicate your boundaries with compassion. Galatians 6:1 encourages gentleness when we are restoring
someone who has been caught up in sin because it's very easy to get
caught up in our own sin when we confront.

How Far Is Too Far?

Many women ask me how far the consequences can go. Some have
even asked me if divorce is an option.

I personally have never considered divorce. Jesus said it is "not what
God had originally intended" (Matthew 19:8 NLT), and God says outright, "I hate divorce" (Malachi 2:16 NLT). But God also hates violence
and abuse. If you fear for your safety or that of your children, the best
advice I can give you is to seek godly counsel from someone who can
advise you based on the specifics of your circumstances.

*But if you are **not** **unsafe**, it is a beautiful decision*
to remain mindfully committed to your covenant vows.

Go ahead and ask me if choosing to stay married to someone broken by sexual sin is evidence of *codependency*.

To answer, I'll turn to the writing of the late Dr. Mark Laaser. (Yes, the same Mark whose wife, Debbie, wishes she'd had disclosure sooner! I told you I had some good news to share about them, remember?)

Mark's battle with pornography started when he was a sweet eleven-year-old boy. By the time he was a married adult, it had escalated into crossing the flesh line. A group intervention, which included his wife, a Christian doctor, and a Christian therapist led him to share the depth of his sin.

After inpatient treatment, years of commitment to professional counseling, and long-standing involvement in community with other recovering men, Mark lived free of sexual sin for more than three decades before he saw the face of his Redeemer. His wife stayed in the marriage, joining him in extensive professional counseling and a community of recovering women. They enjoyed a transformed marriage, celebrating their forty-sixth anniversary before cancer silenced his earthly body.

Here's what Mark had to say about women who choose to stay married to sex addicts:

> Here is a general principle to follow to assess whether or not your decision to stay in the relationship is based on enmeshment/codependency or on a healthy commitment to serve and remain in relationship with your partner. Codependents surrender to and serve their partners out of *weakness*. They are afraid to be alone and feel needy. Healthy partners surrender to and serve their partners out of *strength*. They are secure in themselves and know they could be alone. They choose to be in relationship.[5]

Walk in the strength God has given to you, my friend. Establish boundaries. It's going to enhance your strength in a way you may not have felt before. In fact, I didn't know what to call what I felt when I began asking Bob to observe special boundaries.

What's That Feeling?

When I began to implement boundaries with Bob, I discovered that my heart felt the sadness of this unfamiliar place. But I also felt clarity. It's important that you know I did not feel unattached from my husband, but I did feel more rational. Stronger. Objective.

That's when Tippy told me about *healthy detachment.*

Healthy Detachment · "a feeling of emotional freedom that results when we become more objective about our involvement in a problem or situation with another individual."[6]

You may begin to experience that kind of detachment when you establish and protect holy boundaries with your husband. Detachment includes remaining actively involved in the redemption of the marriage but resigning as the controller of the project. Your spirit finally gets the Truth that you are free to trust in God's sovereignty, and your emotions get the memo too.

(I was once asked if we can see the pattern of detaching in Scripture. I think we can. For example, we read the progression of this emotional change in the book of Habakkuk. The prophet is completely undone and angry at the beginning, but as he relinquishes trust to God, he becomes more objective and more effective as a prophet.)

Before boundaries, my own "strength" showed up as loud and nagging, and there were certainly lots of anger and tears. I was about as effective in relating to Bob as a yippy chihuahua. But when I began to strengthen myself in the Lord and practice boundaries, my demeanor began to look more, well, meek.

And if hearing that word *meek* in the context of setting boundaries sounds strange, let me introduce you to the biblical character quality of meekness. My dear Tippy mentored me in this regard, and I want to pass on what she gifted to me.

It was a game changer for me in my marriage.

Redeeming Meekness

The English definition of *meek* is "quiet, gentle, easily imposed upon."[7] And the world doesn't look at that kind of meekness positively. But biblical meekness is something quite different. And understanding *meek* in the biblical sense can redeem your understanding of the word and make a big difference in your marriage.

The Greek word usually translated "meek" is *praus*. And here's something interesting. Jesus only describes Himself once in Scripture, and He used this word. "I am [*praus*] and humble in heart," He said (Matthew 11:29 NIV).

Praus is apparently a bit difficult to translate. The root "means *more than* 'meek' . . . but rather refers to exercising God's strength under His control." Our English word lacks that sense of strength bonded with gentleness.[8] So here's my own definition for biblical meekness.

Meekness · "a mild, gentle manner, exercising God's strength under His control."

Do you know that the Bible actually communicates that when a husband does "not obey the word" of God, a wife can win him over by being *praus*? Yep! Let's dive into the passage.

First Peter 2, where we find this teaching, is all about suffering. (Fitting, huh?) Verses 21–23 remind us that Christ suffered and did not retaliate nor defend Himself. In fact, He blessed those who cursed Him and submitted to suffering. He was humble, but His humility came from a place of unparalleled strength, not easily-imposed-upon weakness.

In 1 Peter 3, wives are invited to follow Christ's example. God says, let me show you a godly way to respond when you experience suffering in marriage. The chapter starts out with the word *likewise*.

Like what?
Like Jesus!

> **Likewise, wives, be subject to your own husbands, so that even if some do not obey the word, they may be won without a word by the conduct of their wives, when they see your respectful and pure conduct. Do not let your adorning be external—the braiding of hair and the putting on of gold jewelry, or the clothing you wear—but let your adorning be the hidden person of the heart with the imperishable beauty of a gentle [*praus*] and quiet spirit, which in God's sight is very precious.**
> **—1 PETER 3:1–4**

Okay, don't close the book. I realize this passage can be off-putting, to say the least. But I refuse to use a razor blade to cut pieces of my Bible out when they become particularly difficult to understand or apply. This passage was specifically written for Christian wives whose Christian husbands have not been playing inside the fence of God's rules. *You cannot ignore it!*

These verses are actually pretty applicable, if you ask me. For example, "Do not let your adorning be external." Could it be that God knows our go-to strategy is to make ourselves more attractive to hold our husband's attention?

He also knows that doesn't work. Changing you—especially your outer appearance—is never going to be what changes him.

Conduct flooded with meekness—gentle strength— is what will most effectively influence your husband.

I imagine you may be stuck on the words, "be subject to your own husbands." Some versions translate this as "submit yourselves" (NIV), and that *really* sets some people off. But a Greek lesson might be useful here.

The Greek word used here for "be subject" is a form of the verb *hupotasso*. And "its primary meaning is to arrange oneself or to order oneself in such a way that you are helpful to the team. It is a word used in military terms to refer to a formation of soldiers. *Hupotasso* meant to stay in your position in the formation so that everyone can support each other."[9]

God's kingdom is just that—a kingdom, not a democracy. There are positions assigned in the hierarchy. And within the marriage relationship, the husband is designated as head of the household (Ephesians 5:22–24). You and I are called by God to affirm male leadership in our homes and to embrace the position He's assigned to us. To position ourselves so that we are responsive to that leadership and thus helpful to the team.

For a beautiful understanding of what your submission should look like, let's go back to Genesis, where God describes Eve as Adam's *helper*. The original Hebrew Scriptures used the words *ezer kenegdo* to describe that function of womanhood. The word *ezer* means "helper," and the word *kenegdo* means "to accompany." The Bible only uses this kind of language twice to point to a woman's ability to serve and support her husband. The other times these words are used, they point to Someone else in that role: God Himself.[10]

Right now, the Holy Spirit is serving you as your Helper. This places submission in the light of incredible power and strength—*chosen* humility and meekness, not weakness.

How does that operate when you are married to a man whose leadership is broken? Unless you have been there, you can hardly understand how impractical the call to *hupotasso* can seem. But here's a word picture that has really helped me.

I've heard submission in marriage likened to dancing. Both partners utilize their talents and strengths in the dance of marriage, with men leading in sacrificial love and women responding in submission. Well, it's hard to dance with a man whose leadership legs are crippled by sin. It just doesn't work.

When your husband doesn't lead in the dance of life, there's not much to respond to. The dance falls apart.

Here's where it's important to remember that Christian marriage is only a symbol of a greater dance. Let Jesus cut in, my friend. You can safely submit to and respond to Him. Imagine your husband temporarily slinking into a wheelchair between you and Jesus as you continue the dance of headship. Respond to Christ's leadership in the absence of your husband's. Stay in your position.

As a side note, hopefully your husband understands that while he remains crippled by sexual sin, he is not in a condition to lead others spiritually. He may need to resign from any spiritual leadership positions he has, at least for a time.

My husband actually pursued this on his own. He verbalized to me that he was not capable of leading because he'd fallen below the bar of integrity, and he resigned from ministry leadership. The fact that he so willingly submitted to stepping down was a significant gift to me in the middle of a whole lot of pain. It demonstrated to me that he understood the kingdom hierarchy and the fact that because of his sexual sin he was making it messy.

Then one day deep into our marriage work, Bob came to me in humility and asked, "I wonder if you'd begin to let me pray over you every night?"

Tears of joy flooded my eyes, and I imagined Jesus nodding proudly as Bob cut in to dance with me once again.

The man I prayed for became the man I pray with.

My own experience is that boundaries presented in meekness helped me remain in position with the hope that Bob's once-wonderful leadership legs would heal. Setting special boundaries played a significant role in healing my marriage.

Meanwhile, I was able to find other ways to support my husband and give him the respect he needed. For example, while I could not trust my husband to be a spiritual leader when he was struggling with his sexual sin, there were other areas where I could depend on his brain to function well. Business, for example. Bob's a brilliant businessman and a marketing genius. Consulting him as I made decisions for my ministry was one way I could demonstrate and maintain respect for him. Listening and responding to his opinions when we made decisions about our counseling plans was a simple way to remain respectfully engaged.

And the dance went on. As I kept my eyes focused on Jesus as my dance partner, He gave me a general sense of objectivity about Bob's condition (again, healthy detachment). And I think the gentler, less emotional approach to our issues had more power than my previously reactive responses.

Bob's interactions with me became healthier too. Rather than being threatened by my boundaries or feeling rejected, he began to see them for what they were: a form of love.

The first time we spoke about our story was at a Revive Our Hearts event in 2017. My friend Nancy DeMoss Wolgemuth, knowing what Bob and I had walked through, had asked me to speak on loving my husband. And I asked Bob to join me on stage.

I'm glad I did. It was helpful for those women to hear from me, but hearing Bob's heart opened floodgates of hope for them. When he shared there was no doubt that he was still broken by his sin, and he did not minimize it. This single sentence reverberated through the audience:

"I put my wife through hell."

They needed to hear that. It validated and legitimized every tear they had shed. And it rekindled the flame of hope that perhaps one day their husbands would be broken enough to admit the same thing.

Friend, I'm convinced that what Bob said next affirmed that my ability to set boundaries with him was one of the keys to finding healing for his brokenness. He told those women this:

> I've been thinking about how Dannah loves me well . . . partly because I got repeated texts about her speaking on this topic, and she wanted to know if she loved me well.
>
> So I finally sat down and thought about it. This is what I wrote back to her.
>
> "It's not when you cook for me, write me notes, or even when you watch football with me (as cool as that is!)—because people who don't love me will do those things.
>
> "It's not when you say nice things about me, because people who hardly know me sometimes can say nice things.
>
> "And it's not even when you pray for me, because people who detest me can pray for me."

Then Bob looked up at the audience with tears in his eyes and said:

Dannah loves me well when she does whatever it takes to push me toward the often-lonely frontier of God's plan for my life. Dannah loves me well when she does whatever it takes to point out my sin and let me take ownership of it.

In our marriage, loving well means being willing to take the scalpel and open a wound when the disease of sin and selfishness and pride lurk beneath it.

And loving well also means waiting patiently for the right time to start that cut.

My friend, you're gonna need a holy scalpel.

Establishing boundaries with your husband will give you both the healthy parameter you need: a fence to support your creativity, security, and love.

"Need Help Lovin' That Man" is the title of the message Bob and I shared at the Revive Our Hearts event. Use this QR code to find the video on YouTube.

As you work through this part of the book you might want to listen to the *Happily Even After* limited-series podcast. Use this QR code to find and listen in to the one that corresponds to this chapter.

Growing in Intimacy:
Talk to Your Husband about **Boundaries**

Boundaries are not about fixing or punishing each other. They're about living within God's fence of holiness and healthy living. When the boundaries established in God's Word are violated, special boundaries help restore set-apart living as well as emotional and physical safety.

Talk through Truth #3 together:

Boundaries can bring holiness and health to your life.

1. Did your parents (or parent) help you learn the value of boundaries? Were boundaries clear and intact in your family of origin? Did you understand why they existed?

2. Look at the list of biblical boundaries for marriage earlier in this chapter. In which of these do you feel a need to take more personal responsibility?

3. How might establishing some special boundaries help you or your partner feel safe? How could that help you both experience greater holiness?

4. Each of you select one of the boundaries from the list that you sense needs your attention. What special boundary will you personally put into place to protect it? What consequence will you agree to embrace if you do not respect that boundary? Write it down, date it, and put it somewhere that you can both see it.

5. Pray together. Ask the Lord to help you practice and maintain healthy boundaries in your lives.

Everyone says
forgiveness is
a lovely idea
until they have
something to
forgive.

—C. S. Lewis

chapter twelve

Truth #4: Forgiveness Is a Supernatural Act That Produces Freedom

If you hold anything against anyone, forgive them,
so that your Father in heaven may forgive you your sins.
—MARK 11:25 NIV

Bob's big red truck pulled into the driveway. And there in the back were two red leather chairs—the ones we'd been sitting in when Bob confessed his sin to me.

Only a few months ago, I'd asked a teen friend and his brother to move them to the lobby of our ministry offices, where I would not see them as often. Where they would not memorialize my pain.

Today they were bringing them back.

I'd been challenged by my dear friend Amy. She'd immediately forgiven her husband, Wade, when he confessed his sins to her in their pastor's study. The moment had been so powerful that Wade had asked to buy the black sofa they were sitting on.

It was now in their bedroom, a tribute to Amy's forgiving heart.

I'd decided that if God could redeem my marriage, He could surely do the same for two lifeless red leather chairs.

I had come to realize that the behaviors and beliefs that had got us to where we were had to change. What had got us here was not going to get us out. Bob had to learn to live differently. And my pain had to be wrestled with in a manner worthy of a Christ follower. Stuffing the chairs into the corner of an office symbolized what I tended to do with my emotions.

Not anymore.

I calculated the skirmishes my heart would engage in walking by those chairs every day, intending to grapple for victory. My emotions mattered, but they no longer got a final say in how I interacted with Bob.

As the guys began to lift the first red chair out of the truck, I lifted up a simple prayer. It was one I'd needed to say almost daily: "Lord, I choose to forgive Bob."

Sometimes I wish I had a sea of forgetfulness so I wouldn't remember what other people have done to me.

I don't.

But I'm sure glad God does.

The book of Micah depicts God trampling our sin underfoot and then hurling them "into the depths of the sea" (Micah 7:19). He's able to remove our sins "as far as the east is from the west" (Psalm 103:12).

With an ability no human has, God "blots" our transgressions out and says, "I will not remember your sins" (Isaiah 43:25).

Sigh. It would be so nice if we could do that. If we could just forget the ways that other people (like our husbands) have sinned against us, we wouldn't need to struggle with forgiveness.

But struggle we must. Because as difficult as forgiveness is for us mere mortals, it's the only way for you and me to experience true freedom in Christ.

Yep, you read that right.

Forgiveness is not really something you do for your husband. You do it for yourself. It is in your best interest.

When you forgive, you are exercising your strength and your trust in God's power to overcome hatred, anger, bitterness, and victimization. Forgiveness unshackles you from the traumatic event that caused all the pain from the start.

As you've no doubt discovered, however, forgiveness isn't easy. But when you choose to forgive, the Holy Spirit does a supernatural act that produces freedom for you to move on and become whole.

the truth you need *Truth #4: Forgiveness is a supernatural act that produces freedom.*

About twenty years ago, at a time when my own heart needed much redemption, I discovered a prayer process that set me free. I call it Truth prayer. It's a thorough way for two or three people to help one of them identify lies, rip them up, and replace them with God's Truth.

Six Steps to Overcoming Negative Emotions is a limited-series podcast I recorded to teach women this powerful prayer process. Use this QR code to find the series at dannahgresh.com.

I've gone through this process with dozens and dozens of women through the years. Each of them had a deep thirst to experience freedom from something—their past, an addiction, broken relationships, emotional bondage, or even just chronic negative thinking. Watching God set these women free has been quite a learning lab for me. I've made three important observations through the years.

1. Not once have I prayed with a woman seeking freedom who did not have to forgive someone. Our own brokenness and pain are almost always entangled with someone else's.
2. The women who simply would not or could not forgive did not experience freedom in the same magnificent way as those who did. They often remained in spiritual bondage.
3. We all naturally want freedom from our brokenness, but we do not naturally want to forgive!

Today, I want to help you with the *unnatural* part of your redemption journey. Here are four things you need to know about forgiving your husband.

Forgiveness Fact #1:
You Are *Commanded* to Forgive

The Bible communicates it clearly in black and white. Christians are *commanded* to forgive.

> **Put on then, as God's chosen ones, holy and beloved, compassionate hearts, kindness, humility, meekness, and patience, bearing with one another and, if one has a complaint against another, forgiving each other; as the Lord has forgiven you, so you also must forgive.**
> **—COLOSSIANS 3:12–13**

"Put on . . . compassionate hearts"—no room for bitterness!

You'll also need to strap on some kindness, humility, gentleness, and patience. It sure takes a lot of godly garments to equip yourself for the task, doesn't it?

Forgiveness is a task each and every one of us can count on facing. Why? Because "in this world [we] will have trouble" (John 16:33 NIV). That's a 100 percent guarantee. But Scripture tells us specifically that we must press into the hurt that comes our way, *forgiving each other **as the Lord has forgiven us.***

That's the key, of course. The reason we must forgive, according to the Bible, is that forgiving others is inextricably linked to receiving forgiveness from God. Jesus said that directly when He taught His followers to pray:

> "Forgive us our sins,
>   For we also forgive everyone who sins against us."
> **—Luke 11:4 NIV**

The good news, of course, is that God *does* forgive us when we come to Him. And we are commanded to pass on what has been lavishly given to us.

The sad truth is, I'm a rotten sinner. By that I mean I'm *very* good at sinning. So Psalm 130 has become a balm to my guilty heart. Verse 3 reminds me,

> If you, LORD, kept a record of sins,
>   Lord, who could stand?
> —Psalm 130:3 NIV

Not me.

My record would be so long.

Except . . . that sea of forgetfulness. (Thank you, Jesus.)

What would your record look like if it were not for your Redeemer? You are commanded to pass *that* grace—the stuff God applies to your record—on to others. Yes, even to your husband.

Forgiveness Fact #2: Unforgiveness Impacts *You* Negatively

You've heard the old saying that choosing not to forgive someone is like eating rat poison and expecting the rodent to die? Well, turns out that's kind of true.

Stress plays a part in 75 to 90 percent of human diseases.[1] That doesn't mean it can't be useful. A certain amount of stress can come in handy when you're facing a big algebra test or outmaneuvering a charging rhino. It signals your brain and body to respond appropriately. (Study hard! Run!)

When stress works this way to help us it is called *eustress*. But we were only meant to feel that emotion for short durations. When it lasts longer, stress becomes what we refer to as *distress*. And many researchers link physical unwellness—including sleeplessness, reduced immunity for colds and infections, diabetes, heart disease, depression, cancer, and even Alzheimer's to the bad kind of stress.[2] Autoimmune disorders such as lupus are likely related to stress disorders.[3] And pain? Researchers have suggested that chronic pain and stress are "two sides of the same coin."[4]

And here's where forgiveness enters the picture. According to Johns Hopkins Medicine, "ongoing relational conflict" contributes significantly to the experience of distress, but "forgiveness . . . calms stress levels, leading to improved health."[5]

This is from medical research, not Scripture.

But let's take a look at what God's Word says.

> Let all bitterness and wrath and anger and clamor and slander be put away from you, along with all malice. Be kind to one another, tenderhearted, forgiving one another, as God in Christ forgave you.
>
> —Ephesians 4:31–32

The implication here is that forgiveness is tied to a decrease in negative, crippling emotions like anger, bitterness, stress, and guilt. Yes, just as the medical researchers told us.

Refusing to forgive, on the other hand, chains us to the unforgiven person, their sin against us, and all manner of things from the past. I have experienced this in a rather unusual way. I'd like to be vulnerable with you and share my experience.

As you know, I was sexually active as a teenager. That relationship caused no small number of complications in my marriage. As Bob and I sought to experience emotional and physical intimacy, I struggled to fully enjoy both our friendship and our sex life. And—this is important—every time we had a fight, I would think of my former sex partner. Not sexually, but rather in a self-deprecating manner. My mind would teem with untruthful thoughts like, *You'll never be content in your marriage because of your sexual sin.*

I'm convinced, after years of hearing similar stories from other women, that I'm not alone in experiencing this kind of thing. A bond is created when you have sex with someone. This, I believe, is in keeping with Scripture that teaches that a man and wife are made *one* through sexual intimacy. The apostle Paul wrote that this oneness occurs even when the act of sex is a transaction made with a prostitute (1 Corinthians 6:16). Our bodies were created for monogamy.

Biochemistry backs up Scripture in this regard. *Oxytocin* is a neurochemical that washes over a woman's brain when she climaxes sexually. Tender touches, holding hands, kissing, and other intimate forms of contact also stimulate the release of this "chemical of connection" in lower doses. But during orgasm oxytocin floods our brains in generous amounts. This creates a bond that makes us desire intimate contact again and again. And not with anybody but with *the same partner*. Dr. Joe McIlhaney, founder of the Medical Institute for Sexual Health, explains that this

> desire to connect is not just an emotional feeling. Bonding is real because it has become a part of the way one's brain is molded—a powerful connection that often cannot be undone without great emotional pain.[6]

I wish we *only* experienced this kind of brain change when we're married, but it can happen with any sexual partner. And I'm convinced I experienced the fallout from this reality in the early years of my marriage. It prohibited me from being truly emotionally intimate with Bob.

Until I participated in my first Truth prayer session.

My prayer leader asked me to verbalize forgiveness to any past sexual partners. I had only one, but I took time to pray through forgiving him, something I had not previously done. To be honest, I did not think much of it. This was just part of the prayer process, and so I complied.

Months later, however, I realized something glorious! Since that prayer time I had not experienced those self-deprecating thoughts when Bob and I fought. Not once. And to this day, decades later, I have never experienced that again. Forgiveness freed me of that pattern.

Forgiveness is a powerful weapon in the spiritual realm. In fact, the apostle Paul wrote to the church of Corinth and begged them to forgive one another "so that we might not be outwitted by Satan" (2 Corinthians 2:10–11). Don't let Satan win in the battle for your marriage. Forgive!

But don't expect to *feel* like doing it.

Forgiveness Fact #3:
Forgiveness Is Not an Emotion

Many women make the mistake of waiting until they *feel* like forgiving their husband. That's probably never going to happen. Forgiveness is not an emotion. In fact, it's usually counterintuitive to how we feel.

Even so, I've seen women wait for decades to feel ready to forgive, growing more and more bitter each year. Let me see if I can save you some suffering by clarifying what forgiveness is and what it is not.

Here are a few things that forgiveness is:

- **Forgiveness is an act of obedience to God.** When we choose obedience, we are responding to God's forgiveness for our sins and to His requirement that we forgive others as He forgave us (Colossians 3:13).
- **Forgiveness is a tool to clear the conscience.** When navigating a complicated relationship, we can easily get caught up in wrestling with who did what, who is right

and who is wrong, who is guilty and who is to blame. We may even have some guilt of our own to confess. And I don't know about you, but I find it difficult to be present in the moment with my work, the Lord, or my family when I'm distracted by the inner dialogue of defending myself or mentally proving someone else wrong. Do you ever drive down the highway making up speeches to blow your husband out of the water with your anger and wrath? Or are you sometimes tormented with wondering how you may have contributed to the problem? Forgiveness cleans out all that mental clutter. It helps you let go of the wrestling and turn the situation over to God. If you need help praying through those mental conversations, I recommend Psalm 7. That chapter in my Bible is marked up so badly it looks like a toddler has been there. It provides a tremendous pattern to pray when you're working out forgiveness. First, you ask the Lord "if there is wrong in my hands . . . let the enemy pursue my soul and overtake it" (vv. 3–5). You first admit humbly that you want your own heart to be clean before God, but then you invite God to have control of the situation. My conscience is cleaned out when I pray through this chapter of God's Word.

- **Forgiveness is a way that we cancel emotional, spiritual, or material debts rightly owed to us.** Your husband has done significant, costly damage to your marriage and your heart. He may have even run up financial debt to feed his addiction. You are right to feel you deserve justice (or at least some groveling to make things fair). But when you choose to forgive, you are acknowledging that justice is God's job, not yours (Romans 12:17–19). You're accepting that nothing your husband can do will ever be enough to heal your broken emotions. You're letting God take control of anything that needs to be made right.

- **Forgiveness is a promise never to bring the sin up as a tool to hurt your husband.** When your husband confesses his sin to you, he's handing you a nuclear weapon. Don't use it—ever. I'm so thankful that my husband has never used my sinful past against me. Not one time in over thirty years of marriage has he weaponized my disclosure. He is a great forgiver, and because of that I'm able to write this book. His forgiveness is a tool of healing that gave me freedom and courage to minister to precious women like you. Wouldn't you like to be able to say you unleashed something good in your husband by offering him forgiveness?

tell me your story

Before you read on, I want you to take inventory. Look at the "forgiveness is" list in this chapter. Which of these seems most difficult for you? Why? Write a note in the margins of the page where the list appears.

As helpful as it is to know what forgiveness *is*, I think many times women find the courage to extend it when they understand what it does not include. So let's explore a few things that forgiveness is not.

- **Forgiveness is not minimizing, denying, or excusing the wrong that was committed against you.** To truly forgive someone, you need to know what needs forgiving. (Own your damage, remember.) That may seem terribly simplistic, but many women rush to extend superficial forgiveness. There are lots of reasons for this, including longing to move forward in the healing process or receiving well-meaning but poorly informed advice to forgive quickly. I encourage you to take the time you need to understand exactly what your husband has done. God wants your forgiveness to be authentic and complete, not a superficial Band-Aid. Don't let anyone rush you.

- **Forgiveness is not forgetting.** Only God can forget sin. But the fact that we cannot forget has a redeeming quality. You see, if we could forget all the wrongs committed against us and the pain we have experienced, we would not be capable of mercy or empathy for others. I have discovered that God has equipped me uniquely to comfort women who have experienced the kind of pain that I have in my marriage (2 Corinthians 1:3–4). I'm grateful that I can be here for you in your hurt, my friend. I hope you'll pass it on when you are able.

- **Forgiveness is not a single event.** But it does *begin* as an event. At some point you make the decision to forgive. And I hope you schedule a time to verbally express forgiveness to your husband. But because forgiveness is not an emotion, you will find that there are mini events required to follow the big one. Anytime your emotions try to undo the work of forgiveness, you press in. It might be with a little prayer: *Lord, I have chosen to forgive my husband, and I still choose it.* Or it could be decisions you make to keep walking in the direction of forgiveness. My choice to bring my red leather chairs back into my home was an intentional step to keep walking in the direction of forgiveness.

There's a reason forgiveness is not a single event. It isn't easy.

Forgiveness Fact #4:
Forgiveness Is Really Hard—So We Need Help!

Because forgiveness is so very difficult, I am incredibly grateful for God's help. Do you remember that I told you forgiving someone is not natural? If you're having difficulty, the Spirit can help you.

The fact that my friend Amy forgave her husband so quickly and easily had always perplexed me. Honestly, I'd wondered if she forgave her husband prematurely. Some women do, and that only ends up causing additional trauma because they bypass the step of owning their damage.

But when Amy and Wade shared their testimonies with our local congregation, I changed my mind.

Amy had endured horrible sexual abuse in her childhood. It was so bad that she blocked it out of her mind until she was in college and dating Wade.

They were kissing one day when Amy began to manifest a telltale sign of past trauma. Of course, Amy did not notice it, but Wade did.

"Amy," he prodded, "what's wrong? It's like you're not even here when we kiss!"

Amy began to see a Christian counselor, who helped her to learn that she was *dissociating*. That is the clinical term for when people mentally disconnect from themselves and the world around them. Some women, like Amy, experience this when they are intimate with their boyfriends or husbands. It is often a result of childhood sexual abuse. Children generally dissociate when they are abused. And some of them learn that behavior so well that they continue it when they begin to experience sex in marriage.

When it happened to her, my dear friend Amy began the long process of understanding what had happened to her as a child and learning to forgive. I think forgiving an abuser is the hardest and bravest thing a woman will ever do. It requires her to face a vicious battle against shame. And it's a confusing fight since what happened wasn't her fault. Amy spent countless hours in a counseling room reconnecting with the little girl she once was and getting the help she needed to identify lies that the abuse had planted in her heart. One by one she ripped them up and replaced them with God's Truth.

And yes, she learned to stay present and enjoy kissing Wade! They got married and had four beautiful babies.

Then, many years into their marriage, Wade's eyes wandered. His sin broke his heart. And when he confessed it to Amy, years of walking through the valley of shame and building her forgiveness muscle enabled her to see things in a unique way. As her husband sat on one side of a sofa in grief and shame, she saw the spiritual battle for what it was. She saw a little boy who needed help understanding the lies in his heart so he, too, could rip them up and replace them with truth.

Amy knew instantly that she had to forgive Wade. But even she was surprised at how it happened.

"It was like I was picked up off of one end of the sofa, and suddenly I was on the other side wrapping my arms around Wade," she remembers. "I looked him in the eye and told him that I forgave him. It wasn't me. It was Christ in me. It was supernatural."

That I understood!

Forgiving Bob was something I could not do without Jesus. He did it in me. Through me. Let me say this again:

Forgiveness is a supernatural act that produces freedom.

Now I realize some people have a personality that more naturally forgives. And I am mindful that those individuals are not always believers. But in my own life, I do not think I could have accomplished the supernatural act of forgiving Bob without God's help. You, too, may need to rely on God's Spirit within you.

I hope you will choose forgiveness. And that you will trust God to let you know the right time and place for it. For Amy, it happened very early in her and Wade's redemption story. For me, it was slow to come. And I am convinced that the way we expressed forgiveness was right for each of us as unique individuals walking out the unique redemption stories that were unfolding in our marriages.

Don't let anyone tell you forgiveness needs to happen in a certain way. Here's where I get to remind you that recovery work is unique to each couple. Trust the Lord and the advisers He places in your life.

Oh, speaking of trust—forgiveness does not equal trust. That's a whole other battle. So let's talk about it in the next chapter.

As you work through this part of the book you might want to listen to the *Happily Even After* limited-series podcast. Use this QR code to find and listen in to the one that corresponds to this chapter.

Growing in Intimacy:
Talk to Your Husband about **Forgiveness**

Forgiveness is easier for some and harder for others. But God wants us to forgive as we have been forgiven. The cost is great, but Jesus has already paid the price. He wants us to follow His example.

Talk through Truth #4 together:

Forgiveness is a supernatural act that produces freedom.

1. What is your initial reaction to the idea of forgiveness? Is it difficult for you or easy for you? Why?

2. Tell me about a time when someone forgave you. How did that feel?

3. What characteristics of your life might be evidence that you haven't fully forgiven past hurts?

4. Forgiveness is not a one-time event, but it does require an event to get started. If you have already experienced a full confession, you need to proceed with verbalizing forgiveness. Do you feel ready to do this? Why or why not?

5. Pray together. Ask the Lord to make you two great forgivers.

This world and all its brokenness cry out for one thing: a redeemer. That redeemer is Christ, whose forgiving and transforming grace is the only hope for us, our world, and our sexual brokenness.

—Paul David Tripp

chapter thirteen

Truth #5: Trust Is a Gift You Choose to Give

Do you not know that the unrighteous will not inherit the kingdom of God? Do not be deceived: neither the sexually immoral, nor idolaters, nor adulterers, nor men who practice homosexuality, nor thieves, nor the greedy, nor drunkards, nor revilers, nor swindlers will inherit the kingdom of God. And such **were** *some of you. But you were washed, you were sanctified, you were justified in the name of the Lord Jesus Christ and by the Spirit of our God.*

—1 CORINTHIANS 6:9–11

Bob and I squeezed together so both our faces were on the screen. Mike Bivens, our marriage-coach friend from Nashville, had agreed to—as he called it—"coach us up."

"You've got a trust problem," Mike diagnosed confidently.

Bob and I looked toward each other, and suddenly we were a team. "That really doesn't seem right," Bob said.

It was true that we were struggling to communicate effectively with each other. But our commitment lacked no small amount of resolve.

"You're committed to each other—all righty then!" Mike always enthusiastically celebrated what he called our *oneness.* "But here's the deal. I don't think you guys are feelin' it. That's the problem. You gotta put you some deposits in each other's cookie jar!"

"What's that mean?" I asked. Mike was always talking in word pictures.

"Your man has a cookie jar right here." Mike pounded on his chest. "Right there in the middle of his being. And you've got one too. Y'all are not filling up each other's cookie jars!"

That was the day I started calling our marriage-coach friend the Cookie Jar Man.

It would take me a decade to figure out that Bob was actually the one who deserved that title.

Trust in marriage is hard to define. But we sure know when it's lost!

Our energy deflates. And our hearts go on strike. It takes understanding to get them to cross the picket line and engage again.

So let's roll up our sleeves and learn.

Trust · "assured reliance on the character, ability, strength, or truth of someone or something."[1]

Well, in your situation that gets tricky, doesn't it? Let's just consider the word *ability.*

I'll start with a fact we have covered many times: your husband's brain has been hijacked. This compromises his *ability* to be truthful, display character, and be strong.

He may even be at the point where he has trouble concentrating or remembering things, and he might struggle to perform in school or at work.[2] His emotions may also be damaged. Gary Wilson, writing in 2015, stated that almost a dozen studies correlate problematic porn use with depression, paranoid thinking, stress, psychosomatic symptoms, and other mental instabilities.[3]

How do you begin to rebuild trust in a situation like that?

Well, first of all—it does take time. Remember, there's an element of physical healing that needs to take place in your husband's brain. As he detoxes from the chemicals of pornography and sexual sin, he will begin to get control of his thinking once again. Then you and he can begin the process of rebuilding trust.

In this chapter I want to help you reestablish what you might call the cement of your covenant love. Here are four things you need to know about trusting your husband.

Trust Fact #1: The Bible Warns Us Not to Put Our Trust in "Mere Humans"

Didn't expect me to start there? Well, we're told over and over in Scripture that we shouldn't trust each other.

> Don't put your trust in mere humans.
> They are as frail as breath.
> What good are they?
> —Isaiah 2:22 NLT

The Word of God indicates that we can count on some of our most important relationships to fail us. Even a nursing mother whose baby needs her for survival might find herself in a position where she forgets her infant (Isaiah 49:15).

That one always gets me. Can you imagine?

The Bible associates great danger with trusting in mere humans. We put ourselves in position to be cursed, dismayed, and put to shame if we put our trust in other sinful men and women (Jeremiah 17:5-6; Isaiah 20:5). Sorrow awaits the one who trusts in other people (Isaiah 31:1–3 NLT).

Interestingly, behavioral science backs that biblical assessment up. In one longitudinal study of trust in marriage, researchers identified couples whose relationships followed a "zero-sum game pattern"— based on the idea that, in any interaction, "there's a winner and a loser."[4] This means they related to each other in such a way that, in order for one person to "win," or experience trust, the other person had to "lose," or experience betrayal. A simplistic example of this might be a wife who likes to arrive five minutes early to events in order to feel peace and safety. Her husband feels peace and safety when he is not rushed and tends to arrive five minutes late for everything. If this couple is unable to communicate and compromise for one another, they will be bound to a pattern where one of them feels betrayed at all times.

Researchers compared these zero-sum couples to those who demon- strated healthy mutual trust. Well, they tried, anyway. At a certain point the zero-sum-game couples stopped showing up for the research ses- sions. That's because the men were dying![5]

Betrayal is the opposite of trust. When human relationships fail us—as they inevitably do—we experience the trauma of betrayal in the cellular level. Truly, sorrow awaits when we put our trust in other people.

In a sense, though, it's a relief to know I don't have to put my trust in Bob. It lets me take him off the hook and turn to Another for my sense of security and safety: the Lord.

Trust Fact #2: We Are *Commanded* to Put Our Trust in the Lord

You'll read it over and over again in Scripture. The only one you can trust to never let you down is the Lord.

Here's the very first Bible verse I wrote on my index cards when I began collecting Scripture to counsel my heart:

> **Trust in the LORD with all your heart,**
> **and do not lean on your own understanding.**
> **In all your ways acknowledge him,**
> **and he will make straight your paths.**
> **Be not wise in your own eyes;**
> **fear the LORD, and turn away from evil.**
> **It will be healing to your flesh**
> **And refreshment to your bones.**
> **—PROVERBS 3:5–8**

Trust. Lean. These two words may be even more closely related than appears at first sight. To lean suggests neediness, right? Well, one scholar says that the word translated trust means "to lie helpless, facedown."[6] Why would you do that—lean down so far that your nose is to the dirt? Could it be that trust is a way we worship God?

How do you worship Him with your trust?

You trust "with all your heart."

To put part of your trust in God and some in your husband is a complete failure of this invitation to trust the Lord. The Sovereign One gets it all.

What is the outcome when you trust Him that way?

"Healing to your flesh."

"Refreshment to your bones."

When we trust the Lord with all our hearts, our bodies enjoy wellness. Healing. Refreshment.

The beauty of this is not lost on me—a woman whose body was once ravaged with physical symptoms of betrayal trauma and who is married to a man whose brain was impaired by addiction. Oh, we have been and are still a couple who needs healing in our flesh and strength in our bones.

Are you?

Put your trust in the Lord. That is to say, anchor your sense of safety and security to the only one you can rely on never to fail you. God never lies. He will never gossip about you and will never make fun of you. He understands your pain, promises to always be there for you. Faithfulness is part of His character. You can rely on Him.

Always.

Anchoring your heart to God's ability frees you to enter into the energetic task of building healthy relationships that do, in fact, require a measure of trust.

Trust Fact #3: Trust in Marriage Must Ultimately Be Rooted in Trust in God

Although we should never anchor our security in any human relationship, a human relationship still requires a certain level of reliability to work. Evidence of this need could be found by searching the word *trust* on Amazon. I did that today and found over *sixty thousand* books on the topic. Some were about financial trusts or the ability to run a trustworthy workplace. But most of them were about relationships— proof that we value trust in our human interactions. And there sure were a whole lot of books about trust in marriage.

There is no one on planet earth whom either of you can trust the way that you can trust the Lord. Our omnipotent God's ability makes

Him failproof. Your husband will never be completely trustworthy. Nor will you. God is the only one for whom we can have "assured reliance on the character, ability, strength, or truth."

Maybe that's why God's Word never expressly instructs us to trust in our spouses. But it instructs us to trust God over and over.

I'm not saying that trusting your husband doesn't matter. It does. The two of you have entered into a covenant relationship that is meant to reflect the love of Jesus Christ for us. If it is anything, it must be a trustworthy relationship. And Proverbs 31:11 states that a man's heart "safely trusts" in his wife (NKJV). Though it does not command trust, it holds up a reliable relationship as admirable.

But even if you do build a reliable trust in your marriage, your husband will grow old. As will you. Your reliability will fade. And you cannot trust each other not to die.

But you can always trust God.

As you rebuild trust in your marriage, don't make one another the ultimate object of your trust. Instead, pursue trust in God together. The only way I know to do that is to obey God as individuals. Out of that will flow trustworthiness in the marriage.

You cannot control what your husband chooses to do, of course. But what you can do is address your own behavior and hold tightly to the belief that God can use it to influence your husband's choices.

When and if you and your husband reach the point where you both are observing healthy biblical boundaries of marriage, there will be basically three areas where you will both see evidence of trustworthiness.

- **Fidelity.** It's actually one of the Ten Commandments: "You shall not commit adultery" (Exodus 20:14). As I've already stated, you can and should expect this to include avoiding pornography.
- **Honesty.** Also a commandment: "You shall not bear false witness" (Exodus 20:16). That basically means "don't lie."

- **Consistency in behavior.** Matthew 5:37 summarizes this as doing what we say we will do and not doing what we say we won't.

I realize that all of those areas of trust may be compromised in your marriage right now. This leads me to an aspect of trust that cannot be ignored.

Trust Fact #4: Trust in Marriage Is Risky

One definition of trust is "feeling safe when vulnerable."[7] You deserve to feel safe in your marriage, but you must face the reality that it will always be a vulnerable experience.

> To love at all is to be vulnerable. Love anything, and your heart will certainly be wrung and possibly be broken. If you want to make sure of keeping it intact, you must give your heart to no one, not even to an animal. Wrap it carefully round with hobbies and little luxuries; avoid all entanglements; lock it up safe in the casket or coffin of your selfishness. But in that casket—safe, dark, motionless, airless—it will change. It will not be broken; it will become unbreakable, impenetrable, irredeemable. . . . The only place outside Heaven where you can be perfectly safe from all the dangers . . . of love is hell.
> —C. S. Lewis[8]

When Bob and I entered into our marriage covenant, we were making ourselves vulnerable to one another. And both our hearts have been wrung out and broken because of it.

When I had sex as a fifteen-year-old girl, I proved that I'm capable of having sex with someone to whom I'm not married. Not disclosing that to Bob before we were married was a breach of trust. I lied.

He lovingly forgave me.

When my husband consumed pornography and gave his mind over to lustful living, he proved he is capable of violating our marriage vows. He did not provide sexual fidelity.

I forgave him.

At this point, there's really no reason why either of us *should* trust one another. We have exploited one another's vulnerability. And not just in these big things. In little things too.

Many couples do not experience big, traumatic betrayal events. But all couples experience betrayal. It can often be subtle. Not taking the trash out when you agreed that was your weekly chore, saying that you're "just waiting for the Realtor to get back to you" when you didn't send an email as you promised, complaining about your husband in front of your friends—such mini-betrayals can pile up and erode trust.

Find me a couple on planet earth who has not violated trust.

But you can still choose trust for your marriage, even if you must rebuild it. That brings us to our next truth you need:

the truth you need | *Truth #5: Trust is a gift you choose to give.*

Sliding Doors and Cookie Jars

Trusting Bob again was difficult for me, so I told my friend Lynn about my struggle. No one prayed more, cried more, counseled more, and believed in my marriage more than this dear friend. She logged quite a few hours bearing this girl's burden. (She also wins the award for best peanut butter Rice Krispie squares delivered on my saddest birthday ever.)

At one point Lynn invited Bob and me to meet with her and her husband, Dan. They listened and encouraged. And I'll never forget what Dan said to me that night.

"Dannah," said Dan, "Bob certainly hasn't earned your trust. But I'm not convinced anyone really can. *Trust is a gift.* And at some point you just need to decide if that's something you're going to give him."

Being vulnerable and beginning to rebuild trust together after a significant betrayal is a valid choice for your marriage. You should not even attempt it without firmly planting your ultimate trust in God and counting the cost of vulnerability with your husband. But if you're serious about redeeming your marriage, at some point you need to make a deliberate and intentional decision to gift your husband with your trust. But you don't have to do it all at once.

This is where our coaching friend, Mike Bivens, comes in. It turns out the data of behavioral science proves his cookie jar theory to be very useful.

John Gottman, a psychologist who has invested more than four decades of research on divorce prediction and marital stability, believes trust is actually built and rebuilt in the smallest of moments. He calls them "sliding door" moments. The name is based on a movie by the same name. In the opening scene, a woman is running to make the train. She makes it. And her life unfolds. But then the movie replays that scene and she doesn't make it through the sliding door of the train. Her life unfolds in a dramatically different manner.[9]

Gottman says little moments in marriage can be "sliding doors" that change the course of the relationship for good or bad.[10] This could apply to many different aspects of marriage, but it certainly speaks to the process of building—and rebuilding trust.

To put it another way, small, seemingly insignificant acts can put cookies in the trust jar of your heart.

When I heard this, I realized that Bob *had* been rebuilding trust one cookie at a time. I just hadn't realized it.

Below are a few of the decisions I have watched Bob make for the sake of our covenant love. Each choice, large or small, has made a deposit in my "trust fund"—a cookie in my jar. I've written the list in a way that I hope will help you recognize ways that your own husband may be rebuilding trust.

A trustworthy husband

- **confesses his sin with full disclosure and does not minimize or defend his offense.**
- **is willing to answer any questions you have, no matter what.**
- **eagerly establishes and abides by healthy boundaries.**
- is less focused on screens and more emotionally present.
- **humbly accepts any discipline dished out by his spiritual or vocational authorities.**
- **demonstrates an increasing ability to talk about his feelings and needs.**
- **asks to hear about your feelings and needs.**
- **pursues community with other Christian men.**
- **meets regularly with your local body of believers.**
- **stays in counseling until you both mutually agree that the work is done.**
- **is patient with you as you work through the damage his sin has caused.**
- **takes responsibility rather than making excuses when you are triggered.**[11]
- **is attentive to your sexual needs and seeks mutual satisfaction in the marriage bed.**
- **makes change and growth a personal priority in his life.**

- is committed to pursuing covenant love that is steadfast and resilient.
- actively nurtures his relationship with Jesus Christ.

tell me your story

Looking at the "trustworthy man" list, put an x by any of the qualities that your husband is actively living out in front of you. As usually, I've signified with bold type where my husband is demonstrating his trustworthiness. (Just look at all that extra ink!) Do not be discouraged if there is not much evidence of trustworthiness in your husband just yet. We've been working on this a long, long time.

My husband truly has become my Cookie Jar Man. Yours might not be just yet. A cookie jar isn't filled up with trust overnight. We've been working on this for many years and though we're doing a lot better, we're still not perfect. As you can see, a big area of concern for both of us is still the screen time. That's something we both struggle with. My point is that we're still working.

You'll be at this for a long time too. You have to take it day by day.

A Day-By-Day Trust Walk

You may remember that the day Bob confessed his sin to me, I was recovering from a back injury. It was a doozy. I was helping some friends move and hurt myself lifting one of their bags.

I now have a disorder called spondylolisthesis. That fancy name just means that my vertebrae slip out of alignment when I sit for a long time or bend to lift something.

That initial injury changed my life dramatically. The day before the accident I was lifting hay bales on our farm; the next day, Bob was lifting me. At first I could not stand, sit, walk, dress myself, or even use the bathroom without my husband's help. (Where's the embarrassed-face emoji when you need it?) I had to trust Bob for physical stability. For nearly a week he stayed by my side because my ability to perform normal movement was severely impaired by the injury.

But day by day my muscles relaxed from their locked-up trauma response, and I was able to begin physical therapy to strengthen them to do what my bones no longer could. We went on to employ many strategies to return my back to its former ability—time, patience, professional physical therapy, nerve therapy, doctor's visits, multiple mattresses (in search of the right one), x-rays, faithful Pilates training, and commitment. (Today I have a Pilates corset, and I'm proud of it!)

Eventually we were able to trust my back's *ability* to do what it was designed by God to do.

Do you see what I'm trying to communicate about rebuilding trust after sexual sin?

Too many couples rush to trust a man's impaired brain.

You may both desperately want things to go back to normal, but forcing "normal" will result in heartache for both of you. The fastest way to a relapse is to expect too much too soon. Trust really isn't an *either/or* situation. It's more of a continuum. And getting back on the right end of the scale will be a gradual process.

Your husband's brain, his emotions, and his sexual desire can be trained to be trustworthy again. But it will happen *slowly*. Day by day. Week by week. Month by month.

You can and should fully expect him to employ many strategies to restore his sexual integrity. This can include borrowing the strength of your brain, plus time, patience, professional counseling, small-group therapy, doctor's visits, and commitment. You must see this work to believe he is building his sexual integrity muscle back up! Think of them as cookies in your trust jar.

As with all pieces of your recovery, there is no fix-all program that works for everyone. Certainly there are common threads in the way couples rebuild trust, but the process that works for you is your program. Finding it will inevitably be a matter of trial and error—not to mention much prayer and ongoing trust in God.

How do you know when you can fully trust your husband's ability to walk in sexual integrity?

Just as there were signs telling you he was unwell, there will be signs to tell you he is trustworthy. And when you see them, it's time to give the gift of trust.

I'm so thankful for my Cookie Jar Man.

As you work through this part of the book you might want to listen to the *Happily Even After* limited-series podcast. Use this QR code to find and listen in to the one that corresponds to this chapter.

Growing in Intimacy:
Talk to Your Husband about **Trust**

Rebuilding trust in a marriage wounded by betrayal is not impossible, but it takes time and the willingness to work. This is one area where you could really be creative in how you bless and encourage your husband. If he's been taking out the trash . . . that's a cookie in the jar. If he's been paying the bills . . . that's a cookie in the jar. Be lavish with your praise if you are able as you discuss this Truth. It's a great way to put emotional deposits in his heart.

Talk through Truth #5 together:

Trust is a gift you choose to give.

1. What does trust mean to you?

2. Do you agree that trust is a gift? Why or why not?

3. Think about a time when you didn't feel you could trust your spouse. What could he or she have done to make you feel safe enough to offer the gift of trust?

4. What do you need from your spouse right now in order to trust him or her more?

5. Pray together. Ask God to give you a greater sense of trust in Him to guide your life and redeem your marriage.

Sex is not a consumer good; it's a covenant good.

—Tim Keller

chapter fourteen

Truth #6: Intimacy Is about Sharing Your Whole Self with Your Spouse

My beloved is mine, and I am his.
—SONG OF SOLOMON 2:16

"We don't really have sex very often." A sweet missionary looked into my eyes. What a privilege to be a safe place for her.

It had now been a few years since Bob and I walked through our own shame and pain. The redeeming work of Jesus was beginning to include the opportunity to counsel others. And I was finding that very often the place they needed God to show up with some healing was their marriage beds.

I asked this dear woman what got in the way of her and her husband wanting to have sex.

"Nothing specific," she began, then changed course. "Or I guess everything. Traveling, ministry, the kids! It all gets in the way, and I think we've both just resigned ourselves to think we've had enough sex."

It always makes me sad to hear women say things like that, but I prayed for the right words to encourage this dear woman of God.

"Your marriage is a picture of Christ and the church," I challenged gently. "Perhaps sex could be likened to your prayer life? Will you ever grow close enough to the Lord that you say, 'Aw, I've had more than enough prayer! Don't think I'll make time for that any longer.'"

A lightbulb went off in my friend's head. I could see it in her face!

Intimacy is at the heart of God's intention for sexual expression. The Old Testament uses the word *yada* for sex between a husband and wife. Its basic meaning is "to know," although it can also carry a sense of "to be made known" and even "to reveal oneself."[1] God's very definition of the act of marriage transcends the physical and emphasizes an emotional knowing.

Sadly, our culture is obsessed with the physical aspect and practically ignores the emotional. How ridiculous this must be to the Designer of sexual intimacy!

Imagine I took you into a dark room, but I brought a lamp. When I plug it in, do you become obsessed with how the pins on the plug connect into the outlet? Or are you grateful for the warm, comforting light the lamp produces? Of course, you know what to be excited about.

When it comes to sex, so many in our culture don't know what to be excited about. We tend to be mostly concerned with how things plug in rather than with the warmth and comfort of intimate relationship.

A sexual addict experiences this confusion to a severe degree. He has become so obsessed with the mechanics of sex that he has disabled his ability to be intimate.

As you and your husband work together to rip up the lies in his belief system, it's so important to cultivate truth to replace those empty spots. If you rush to be sexual with him when he's detoxing from lustful thinking, you'll miss a wonderful opportunity to properly develop emotional intimacy with him, which is about much more than plugging—well, you know how it works!

What I'm about to share with you is very important. Remember, a man who is struggling with porn or sex addiction probably has an intimacy disorder. That may well mean he either avoids sex with you or limits it to a quick act of physical release, leaving you hurt, lonely, angry, and frustrated.

Believe me, that's not what God had in mind when He designed sexual intimacy.

the truth you need *Truth #6: Intimacy is about sharing your whole self with your spouse.*

True sexual intimacy requires that both partners live in sexual integrity, which has been defined this way:

> My sexual choices are a consistent expression of my relational and spiritual commitments.[2]
> —Dr. Juli Slattery

Think about that! It could also be put this way:

> To have physical union without having
> whole-life union is a lack of integrity.[3]
> **—Tim Keller**

Our marriages and our sexuality display the love of Jesus Christ when they are an authentic extension of our covenant commitment.

Consumer Good or Covenant Good

If you want to redeem your thinking about sex in thirty-four minutes, listen to a sermon by Tim Keller titled "Love and Lust." In it he says that authentic sex is a *covenant good*. By that, Keller means that sex is sacramental. Just as regularly partaking of communion is a way of remembering our Redeemer's new covenant, authentic sex is a way to acknowledge our marriage covenant.

> A sacrament is an external, visible sign of an invisible reality. . . .
> When you use sex inside a covenant, it becomes a vehicle for
> engaging the whole person in an act of self-giving and self-
> commitment. When I, in marriage, make myself physically naked
> and vulnerable, it's a sign of what I've done with my whole life.[4]

Keller says many people outside of marriage get into the pattern of using sex as a *consumer good*. You take rather than give. Sex is about what excites *you*, what it does for *you*, and who is attractive to *you*. The act itself is thus cut off from any whole-life commitment. Sex becomes a tool you use to get what you want, not an extension of what you're doing to give your life to someone. It is more than likely limited to the physical and lacks true intimate friendship.

I think many married couples fall into such consumeristic patterns in their sex lives. If it is a commodity you withhold or offer to ma-nipulate emotions, decisions, or moods, you're using it as a consumer good, not a sacramental covenant good. When sex becomes rushed, obligatory, or disconnected, you're just using it to scratch an itch or to avoid conflict with your partner. Your time in bed is relegated to merely physical function when it lacks eye contact, intimate communication, laughter (because, hey, it doesn't always work out just so), and expression of gratitude.

The Samaritan woman Jesus met at the well in John's gospel knew what it meant to treat sex like a consumer good. She came to the water hole alone because of, well, shame (John 4:7–29). Sexual memories, divorces, rejections, and pain from men had created a thick wall of isolation for her. She came for water in the heat of the day because no one would talk to her. She was that sexually broken.

And why was Jesus there? John 4:4 says He "had to pass" through Samaria on His way to Galilee, but actually He didn't. It was not common for Jews to choose this route due to their disdain of Samaritans.[5] But compassion pressed Jesus to go meet this woman.

My friend, Jesus will meet you where you are too. He will talk to you in your brokenness just as He talked to that hurting woman. He is not afraid of your secrets nor your husband's sins. And He doesn't suffer small talk.

"Bring me your husband," Jesus told the Samaritan woman (verse 16). He got right to the topic: her spiritual and emotional thirst. Never satisfied, she was going from man to man to consume what she thought she needed.

But Jesus knew what she was really thirsty for. It was something that only He could give her: living water. He was—and is—both the Source and the Living Water itself.

In 1945 the novelist Bruce Marshall wrote that "the young man who rings the bell at the brothel is unconsciously looking for God."[6] He was describing the same dynamic that Jesus saw in the Samaritan woman.

That our thirst for sex is really a misdirected thirst for God. And that until we quench our thirst with Living Water, we're not likely to find fulfillment anywhere else.

The Power of a Fast

Sometimes when my appetites are not directing me to Jesus, I practice the spiritual discipline of fasting. I find that denying myself food or limiting my intake to liquids or vegetables helps me reset my desires and focus on the ultimate Source of my satisfaction and fulfillment. Invariably, this dynamic flows into every area of my life. When I control my rogue eating, my spiritual and emotional life thrives. Most importantly, it helps reacquaint me with my passion for my Redeemer.

Many couples find this same principle helpful when it comes to redeeming their marriage after sexual sin. Ironically, they discover that the best way to pursue whole-self intimacy may include *not* sharing their bodies with one another for a time.

Many counselors and recovery programs recommend such a period of abstinence while a husband "dries out" from his dopamine overload. This gives the couple a wonderful opportunity to retrain their minds and bodies to include emotional intimacy in the physical act of sex and for God to redeem the way you both experience and view sex. The sexual fast helps them reset their intimacy with one another and with the Lord.

You may decide, along with your counselor or a program you participate in, to embrace a season of sexual abstinence. I highly recommend that you approach it biblically. And yes, the Bible actually has something to say about this:

> Do not deprive one another, except perhaps **by agreement for** a limited time, that you may devote yourselves to prayer; but then come together again, so that Satan may not tempt you because of your lack of self-control.
>
> **—1 Corinthians 7:5**

If you choose to fast from sex, it is important that you and your husband mutually agree to do so. And you should indeed devote yourself to prayer for the duration of it. Take the time to drink deeply of the Living Water.

This time of abstinence is not without benefits to you. Your sex life is probably in need of some nurturing. Many wives of addicts say that their marriage bed is plagued by things like:

- avoidance or a lack of interest in sex
- frustration over the transgressive things he wants to do
- erectile dysfunction for him or difficulty achieving orgasm for her
- insecurity about how her body compares to what he's seen
- pain during sex
- viewing sex as an obligation; not enjoying it
- emotional disconnection during sex

The purpose of abstaining from sex is *not* to avoid sex, even though that will be part of it. In fact, if you're relieved at the idea, you know what to pray about. God wants you to enjoy a fulfilling sexual relationship with your husband. I believe you can have that, but your brain has to be engaged for it to happen. Spend some time praying for a desire to make love to your husband.

If you're *not* too happy about this idea, I understand. Desiring sexual intimacy with your husband is good. Enjoying sex is healthy and godly. Spend some of your time praying that your husband's desire would match yours and that God would use your sacrifice to help your husband desire sexual intimacy with you.

tell me your story

Okay, you know the drill by now. Which of the listed issues have been a problem in your sex life? Forgive me if I don't mark Bob's and my challenges in bold this time. I have a conviction about keeping what happens in our bedroom private between the two of us!

The purpose of this time *is* to build emotional intimacy. How you do that will depend on where you are in your redemption story.

It could be that you'll work independently to understand what's happening in your marriage. It's completely okay to do this at the beginning of your work when you both need a little space to think through things and become educated. If you're at this point in your recovery work, you should seek some accountability from a godly woman who will keep your heart open to your husband.

Or perhaps you're at a place where you're ready to work together. For you, abstinence can be a way of creating safety in the relationship as you build nonsexual intimacy. You might go for long walks together, share hobbies or other activities, or just spend quality time talking. But these activities should not end in sex. Instead, you need to focus on your friendship.

When the agreed-upon time for your sexual fast has come to completion and you are ready to reengage sexually, I'd advise you to take it slowly. Focus on learning to be emotionally and spiritually present to each other during sex. Reframing your view of sex to align with God's design is an important step for both of you.

Here's a simple way to ensure that your sex is emotionally intimate. Spend time talking and connecting for an hour or so before you have sex. (I think that's called a date.) Flirt with each other. Listen to each other. Look into one another's eyes. Avoid the temptation to rush through a physical encounter and let your intimacy lead to something more holistic.

If you can participate in a short time of abstinence with your husband, you'll be helping him move forward with the goal of having *sexual integrity*.

Pursuing Sexual Integrity

Sexual integrity is not just avoiding sex outside of your marriage covenant. It also includes enjoying healthy sex within it. As you move forward to be intimate with your husband, you want to move forward in a way that is good for both of you.

I was talking to my friend Dr. Juli Slattery about this book, and she broke a biblical sexual ethic down into two core commitments.[7]

Commitment #1: We don't engage in sex outside of marriage.

This commitment to sexual faithfulness certainly includes not having sex with anyone else (Exodus 20:14; Matthew 5:28). But the Bible also references other kinds of infidelity that could be harmful to your relationship with God and with your husband:

- **Impurity**—letting yourself be defiled or degraded, especially by the surrounding culture. The New Testament has several words for this. *Akatharsia* (Galatians 5:19 and others) refers to "lustful, luxurious, profligate living."[8] *Molusmos* (used once, in 2 Corinthians 7:1) references "the corruption of morals, principles or character."[9] *Rhuparos* (James 2:2; Revelation 22:11) refers to being "dirty" with "moral filth."[10] Obviously, there are many ways this could apply to living in our sex-saturated culture.

- **Lustful passions**—unrestrained, indiscriminate sexual desire for men or women other than the person's marriage partner (Mark 7:21–22; Ephesians 4:19). This could include pornography or giving way to an obsessive sexual mindset.
- **Obscenity and coarse jokes**—sexual humor (Ephesians 5:3–4).

Do you get the picture? Committing to faithfulness in marriage means that all sexual thoughts, desires, and impulses should drive you to your marriage bed or be shut down.

Commitment #2: We make sexual intimacy a priority within marriage.

We fall short of aligning our sexual and spiritual lives if we only focus our sexual ethic on what we should not do. God's rules about sex are not one big "thou shalt not!" A biblical sexual ethic also takes care to observe what God instructs we *should* do, and Scripture speaks to mutually satisfying and frequent sexual pleasure between a husband and wife. Passages like Proverbs 5:18–19 and the entire Song of Solomon celebrate the gift of marital sexual pleasure—and so should we!

Check this out as well:

> The husband should fulfill his wife's sexual needs, and the wife should fulfill her husband's needs.
> **—1 Corinthians 7:3 NLT**

We are called as husbands and wives to minister to one another sexually. This takes time and commitment. In fact, in the Old Testament a newly married man was not supposed to go to war or do business for a whole year so that he could "bring happiness to the wife he has married" (Deuteronomy 24:5 NIV).

Do you think what made her happy in that first year was helping her with the dishes!?

Wifely Happiness 101

Speaking of happiness, many women ask me for advice about what's okay in the bedroom—often because what has been taking place has not been comfortable for them. This is a great time to change that. If you are not comfortable with specific things your husband wants to do in the bedroom, it's important to talk about it with him so you can come to a mutual agreement. As I stated briefly in the chapter on boundaries, I believe that if 1 Corinthians 7:5 says we can mutually agree to abstain, it is also logical that we should arrive at mutual agreement on what constitutes enjoyable and healthy sex.

This is where things get fuzzy, though. We don't see anywhere in the Bible where God clearly says no to things like masturbation, sex toys, or oral sex. Does that mean that mutually masturbating one another is okay? Can you use sex toys if it brings greater pleasure to both of you? Is oral sex okay?

You'll find very different opinions from Christian leaders on these topics that are not directly mentioned in the Bible. I feel firmly convicted that we must be careful not to create legalistic rules about things God does not condemn. He created sex for pleasure, and we teach an incomplete theology of sexual integrity if we do not allow room for creative pleasure inside of marriage.

The Corinthian church had questions about the same kinds of things that you and I do. Instead of giving them hard and fast rules on these gray areas, Paul gave them guidelines on how to use good judgment when the Bible doesn't clearly state something as right or wrong.

> "I have the right to do anything," you say—but not everything is beneficial. "I have the right to do anything"—but I will not be mastered by anything.
> —**1 Corinthians 6:12 NIV**

A few chapters later Paul essentially repeats himself, so he must have felt this advice was important:

> "I have the right to do anything," you say—but not everything is beneficial. "I have the right to do anything"—but not everything is constructive. No one should seek their own good, but the good of others.
> —**1 Corinthians 10:23–24 NIV**

When you are not sure whether something is okay in the bedroom, I suggest putting it through Paul's filter:

- **Is this beneficial?** Is it good for me? For my spouse? Is it good for our marriage?
- **Does it master me?** Can it be habit-forming or addictive?
- **Is it constructive?** Does it help me grow and mature? Does it build our marriage?
- **Is it loving?** Does this action show love toward others, or is it selfish?

There's no reason why you cannot cover your bodies in chocolate sauce and have a delicious time together. (In fact, if you take your cue from Song of Solomon, that is quite biblical!) But you must put everything through the filter of God's Word together and determine mutually how you as a couple can find sexual happiness and fulfillment.

In addition, you must be compassionate about one another's sexual history. Sometimes actions that seem like a perfectly normal and natural part of foreplay will trigger a man or woman who was abused as a young person. This is an opportunity for intimate communication and mutual problem-solving. You may need to find ways of relating sexually that are equally pleasing and less emotionally painful. Or you may be able to (gently) work through the pain until something that once was triggering becomes enjoyable. I have talked with women who have experienced both of these beautiful outcomes.

What about anal sex? As I've said before, many women ask me for advice on this topic. Usually, it is because their husband wants to have anal sex but they do not.

There are good reasons why these women do not enjoy this. Tearing, bleeding, and infections are common consequences of misusing a part of the body meant to be an exit. Because of this, even many secular medical organizations advise against anal sex and encourage other, more beneficial expressions of physical intimacy. So I believe you can confidently go to your husband and communicate to him that you no longer want that particular action (or any problematic form of sexual expression) to be a part of your bedroom activities.

Even while you're establishing such sexual boundaries, assure him that you want to find other ways that you can experience mutual pleasure. I know that's not always easy. A woman's body and emotional makeup are complex. It often takes patience, communication, a sense of safety, and a lot of practice for a man to help his wife achieve orgasm. (Do you think maybe God designed it that way to safeguard the emotional connection?)

Sometimes the challenges of enjoying sex or achieving orgasm could result from early abuse (as stated above). It could also come from having had rushed and hurried sex as a teen or college student. Sometimes it's directly related to your husband's problem with sexual sin—his previous disinterest in sex with you or your fear that he is comparing your body to things he has seen online (or elsewhere). And sometimes it's just because you've both been treating sex as a physical act and not involving your emotions. Whatever has caused the issue, there is a great chance that you and your husband can find ways to successfully address it together.

Though I hesitate to be this vulnerable, I want you to know that my own body needed some retraining. I think my problems may have been a result of several factors mentioned above. But when I finally realized how important it was to my husband that sex was mutually enjoyable, I researched options for us to retrain my body to respond to Bob. We quickly learned that we could either let the suggested exercises be a burden, or we could make them fun. So we chose to have an absolute blast learning.

There are some excellent books that can help you to do this for yourself. I've listed them at the end of this chapter. If they don't help, Christian sex therapy could be both helpful and fun.

Many men communicate that the most exciting thing about sex is producing pleasure for their wives. I hope you will approach your marriage bed with an enthusiastic mindset.

God's Word communicates a positive attitude about your sexual desires. You can have that too. And you should.

Give your whole self to your spouse. And expect to receive all of him in return.

As you work through this part of the book you might want to listen to the *Happily Even After* limited-series podcast. Use this QR code to find and listen in to the one that corresponds to this chapter.

Growing in Intimacy:
Talk to Your Husband about **Sexual Intimacy**

Sexual intimacy includes enjoying the physical act of sex and experiencing it in the safe context of friendship. You'll find that this ebbs and flows due to many factors in life, but the biblical call for married couples to minister to each other in the bedroom remains.

If you do not feel you are able to do that yet, that's okay. But be sure you have a Christian counselor advising you and holding you accountable to make wise decisions in this area. Sexual intimacy is an important part of your love relationship.

If you are ready to work on this but feel stuck, I'm hoping this conversation will help get you unstuck. If it doesn't, seek help together.

Talk through Truth #6 together:

Intimacy is about sharing your whole self with your spouse.

1. Do you think the concept of mutual sexual abstinence is something that could help you reset your sexual intimacy? Why or why not?

2. If you participate in a time of sexual abstinence, how long should it be?

3. What do you enjoy about your sex life? What do you wish you could change?

4. Pray together. Ask the Lord to protect your sexual intimacy and give you wisdom to practice it well.

recommended reading

- *The Gift of Sex: A Guide Sexual to Fulfillment* by Clifford and Joyce Penner. Includes exercises to overcome sexual barriers.
- *God, Sex, and Your Marriage* by Dr. Juli Slattery. Guides you in rethinking your understanding of sex.

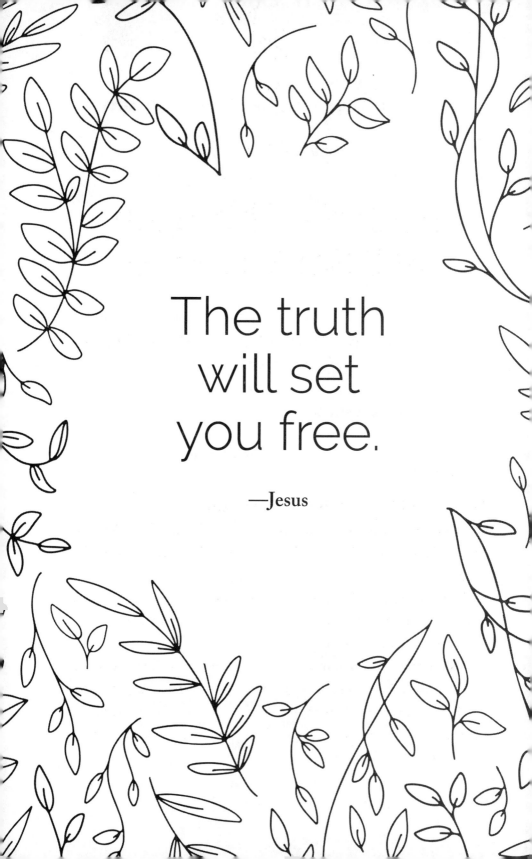

The truth will set you free.

—Jesus

chapter fifteen

Truth #7: The Truth Will Set You Free

For freedom Christ has set us free; stand firm therefore,
and do not submit again to a yoke of slavery.

—GALATIANS 5:1

Spring 2020.

I sat glued to the television screen.

"Half the world's population is under some form of lockdown to reduce the spread of the virus that causes COVID-19," announced a talking head.

Bob walked into the room talking on his phone. "Hang in there, man," he said sadly, then slipped his iPhone onto the kitchen table.

"Someone else get it?" I asked.

"Nope. That was one of the guys," he answered. That's what he called the men in his support group, the ones who held his feet to the fire in accountability. Years into recovery, my man was still faithfully attending the group. I knew some of the guys but not most of them. I was grateful for all of them.

"He sounded absolutely terrified," Bob said.

"Of the virus?" I asked.

"No . . ." Bob answered slowly, careful not to disclose anything confidential. "He's . . . um . . . well, new to the group. He doesn't know how his marriage will ever survive being cooped up at home together."

My eyes grew wide with realization. I hadn't thought about marriages in the early stages of recovery being locked down together. That had to be difficult.

Bob and I were secretly having a blast in lockdown. Like school kids on snow days, we relished the change of pace and the time alone together.

"He's not the first one to tell me that," he continued. "A lot of the guys resent being stuck with their wives."

Then Bob Gresh said something that actually made my heart flutter: "All I could think was I'm so incredibly happy to be stuck here with you!"

And he was.

We were.

And we still are.

Is it happily ever after? No matter what the world's romantic deceptions tell us, that's not an achievable goal in marriage—or in life, for that matter.

But I'm here to tell you that Bob and Dannah Gresh are actually living in what you might call happily even after. In recent years our covenant love has thrived—a sweet testimony to God's redeeming work in our life.

Here's a dose of reality for you from the words of Jesus Himself:

"I have said these things to you, that in me you may have peace. In the world you will have tribulation. But take heart; I have overcome the world."
—JOHN 16:33

Not the power verse you expected at the end of this book?

Look closer.

There's a truth here that's more powerful than the fact that marriage—and life in general—is hard.

Jesus said, "Take heart."

That means, "Be confident."

Be confident of what? "I have overcome the world."

The original Greek puts some chutzpah and some hope into this admonition. The Greek word *nenikeka* is used here for "overcome." It's a form of the root word *nike*—yes, as in shoes!—and means "to be victorious over." But it's the *perfect tense* of this verb that tells us something vital. It "describes *a completed action in the past* that has *continuing impact in the present.*"[1]

Quite simply, that means we have a Redeemer who is still at work.

Jesus' death on the cross won and *is still winning* this battle in your marriage. The worst of the world's trouble has no eternal impact on your story. Sin and death *have lost* and *are losing* their grip.

Jesus, God's own Son, is not finished overcoming. He's left His precious Holy Spirit here to help us until His work on earth is done. And one day it will be.

But probably not today.

So before you close this book, I want to briefly touch on the belief that will make the biggest difference in your marriage and in your life. I've actually been referencing this concept all along, but I've saved the big reveal for last because it matters most.

Here's the final truth you need:

the truth you need 〉 *Truth #7: "The Truth will set you free."*

Those aren't my words. They come from Jesus Himself. And believe me, they work. I want to tell you about a special potency that this world needs to see you and your husband experience.

But before I tell you what it is, let's review something.

We all sin or have unhealthy emotions because we have believed a lie. And, oh, is there sin trouble in our broken world! I believe that's because as a society, we have made lies our refuge. I know I've said that a time or two, but I want to land on it one more time from a different perspective.

Culture Has Made a Lie Our Refuge

Just as the nation of Israel once slid slowly into sin and rebellion, so has our Western world. We have truly "made lies our refuge and falsehood our hiding place" (Isaiah 28:15 NIV), especially when it comes to our view of sex.

The so-called sexual revolution promised freedom and happiness, but it has only produced spiritual and emotional bondage to addiction and pain. According to Pastor John Mark Comer, it's all Sigmund Freud's fault.

> The tipping point was Freud. While I'm not a psychologist, most of my psychologist friends tell me that, savant that he was, Freud got pretty much everything wrong, and yet many of his ideas created the cultural air we now breathe. Prior to Freud, most people in the West (whether they knew it or not) thought about desire through the lens of the fourth century philosopher Augustine.[2]

Imagine the beliefs of Saint Augustine of Hippo being the ones our culture embraced! While a little research will reveal that this early Christian theologian faced his own battles with lust, he eventually turned to Truth. He is considered by some theologians to have influenced more Christian thinking than anyone other than the apostle Paul.

Augustine believed that the basic problem of humanity was disordered desires. In other words: *sin*. According to theologian Matt Jenson, he was probably the first to formulate a view of sin known as *homo incurvatus in se*, or "humanity curved in on itself."[3] This idea that sin is essentially self-centeredness was later expanded by Martin Luther and other theologians.

Not so long ago, Augustine's biblical philosophy had Western culture in a position to seek the highest good—love—first and foremost and to quiet lesser desires like sex. But Freud believed that *sex* was our most important desire. The founder of psychoanalysis expressed nothing short of rancor for Christianity.[4] His life's goal seemed to be to override historic Christian values, which he successfully did by placing us on a conveyor belt to make a lie our refuge.

Dr. Alfred Kinsey took Freud's view one step further by declaring that sexual behavior the culture had once deemed immoral was actually normal behavior that needed to be expressed freely. In a sense, his books *Sexual Behavior in the Human Male* (1948) and *Sexual Behavior in the Human Female* (1953) ushered in the destruction of our nation's moral framework.

The late Dr. Judith Reisman, a recognized historian in human sexuality, revealed that Kinsey's research involved systematic child sexual abuse under the guise of science.[5] His studies even involved a Nazi pedophile who had recorded the sexual responses of children between the ages of two months and fourteen years.[6] This so-called "research" is the foundation of the sex education in today's American education system from elementary school through postgraduate studies.[7]

In 1949, a twenty-two-year-old college virgin, Hugh Hefner, read Kinsey's *Male* volume and determined to take the philosophy to the masses. He launched *Playboy* magazine in 1953. He once said, "Kinsey was the researcher and I am his *pamphleteer*."[8]

Since the 1960s, when the sexual revolution provided traction for these philosophies, it's been a slippery slope of sex lies.

I'm afraid you and I are sitting in the aftermath.

And how's that working for us?

"Happiness levels have been in decline since, interestingly, the '60s."[9]

We live in a society of sin slaves who do not even know what placed them in spiritual bondage. That's because they have been educated to view sin as good.

No one knew that more than the two men who spent their lives selling us the lie.

There is quite a bit of evidence that both Kinsey and Hefner lived unhappy lives. Some researchers believe Kinsey died of a slow and painful sickness called *orchitis*, a swelling in the genitals possibly caused by years of self-inflicted sadomasochism as well as STDs.[10] As for Hefner, he died alone and afraid, having experienced a loveless sex life with little to no intimacy.[11]

It doesn't seem like these men found happiness in their sex lives.

But they remained impostors to the end—the epitome of 2 Timothy 3:13, which warns us that "evil people and impostors will go on from bad to worse, deceiving and being deceived." Their stories provide clear testimony that Satan's lies lead to destruction.

The devil's "only" intentions are to "steal and kill and destroy" (John 10:10). In spite of the evidence of this in their lives, Kinsey and Hefner succeeded in producing a culture where there is a social cost to speaking out against the cult of pornography and sex without boundaries.

Truly, we as a culture have made a lie our refuge.

But there is one thing more powerful than lies—God's Truth. So let me remind you how vital it is that you and your husband work together and with biblically based, clinically informed individuals to figure out what lies are festering in your belief system. And then dive into God's Word to find the Truth to counter those lies.

Get Truth-Full!

You can live in freedom. Your husband can too. Our Redeemer spoke these words to tell you how.

> "If you abide in my word, you are truly my disciples, and you will know the truth, and the truth will set you free."
> —John 8:31-32

I repeat: *you* can know the Truth. And it *will* set you free.

How can you know it? By *abiding* in God's Word.

To "abide" means to stay. Jesus is inviting you not to be pulled away from Truth by the world's lies but instead to persistently remain in a mindset of Truth.

And how do you do that?

Get so full of the truth that there's no room for the lies!

This, my friend, brings us full circle to the tools I've been encouraging you to use all along. They're actually spiritual disciplines. And practicing them is how you keep yourself full of truth.

Do you recall what tools of redemption I invited you to pick up and use at the beginning of this book?

- **Prayer.** It's your weapon (James 5:16)!
- **The Bible.** It's the light for your path (Psalm 119:105).
- **Community.** Your sisters in Christ will provide guidance and keep you from isolation, one of Satan's favorite weapons. As they carry your burden—and you theirs— you'll fulfill the law of Christ (Galatians 6:1).
- **The Lord.** He is the only One capable of strengthening you for this epic battle with evil. And He promises to hold you up when you feel weak (Isaiah 41:10).
- **Covenant Love.** God's unfailing love is the only remedy for sin. Knowing it will equip you with everything you need to do His will, including loving your husband (Hebrews 13:20–21).

These are not the world's trailblazing modern tools of recovery, but ancient tools Christ followers have been successfully employing for centuries. Using them is what enables you to discover and remain in the Truth of God's Word. Don't put them down when you close this book. I urge you to employ them each and every day.

In addition to those foundational disciplines, there are others, some of which we have explored:

- **Stewardship.** You've got to take care of your own heart, mind, and soul. No matter who does the damage. It is an act of worship to let the Holy Spirit transform your mind and to present your body to God (Romans 12:1–2).
- **Lamentation.** It is your sinless, perfect response to the brokenness in our world (John 11:35).

- **Sabbath.** We're commanded to practice a rhythm of rest, which our bodies, souls, and spirits sorely need (Exodus 20:8–11).
- **Submission.** Think of it as chosen humility and meekness to the redemptive mission of Jesus Christ. It causes the devil to run from you (James 4:7)!
- **Confession.** When you drag your sins into the light, you will be healed (James 5:16). And you will have intimate fellowship with God and other believers (1 John 1:7).
- **Forgiveness.** This is both a command (Colossians 3:13) and a supernatural act that produces freedom in your heart (Matthew 6:14).
- **Fasting.** Some battles simply won't abate until you humble yourself and acknowledge the power of the Holy Spirit by temporarily abstaining from food, drink, or other normal behaviors (Matthew 17:21 NKJV).
- **Sexual Abstinence.** This of course is a specialized kind of fasting where you and your spouse mutually agree to abstain from sexual activity for a time. What an opportunity to exercise your self-control through the power of the Holy Spirit (Galatians 5:22–23). It's also a way to retrain your brains to conform the way you think about the act of marriage to God's definition (1 Corinthians 7:5).

Practicing these spiritual disciplines will put you in position to know the Truth and experience freedom. But be warned: perfunctory execution of these disciplines leads only to legalism, not freedom.

The point of any spiritual disciplines is not to do them. It's to *know* Truth.

And Truth is a person.

Unless you become intimate with Jesus Himself, you'll never experience freedom.

Your Story Is Your Greatest Asset

Let's revisit the story of the Samaritan woman that Jesus met at the well. The one who'd tried to find her happiness in man after man but never did.

Then she met Jesus, who is not just the Living Water but also the Truth that sets people free. He told her, "Whoever drinks the water I will give them will never thirst. Indeed, the water I give them will become in them a spring of water welling up to eternal life" (John 4:14 NIV).

And that is what happened. The Samaritan woman became an overflowing well of eternal life.

She dropped her jar, a representation of drinking from the well of sexual desire. (Oh, that God would cause so much joy in your husband's relationship with Jesus that he drops his jar!) And then this woman who had come to the well alone so people would not remember her lifestyle ran through the town saying, "Come see a man who told me everything I ever did!"

What radical vulnerability! The woman's shame was erased, and she knew her story was now worth telling.

John 4:39 tells us that "many Samaritans from that town believed in [Jesus] because of the woman's testimony." Quenching our own thirst with the Living Water always leads to the quenching of other thirsty people.

That's true for you too. Your story is your greatest asset in God's kingdom. Not the picture-perfect, plastic-covered pages that some present, but the ones covered in the dirt of sin and no small amount of the blood of Jesus. The pages you're living in right now, my friend.

Many people believe that sexual sin is one of the greatest threats to Christianity. According to a study completed by Josh McDowell, 60 to 72 percent of men in our churches can be classified as sex addicts.[12] The damage is especially devastating as pastors and Christian leaders are discredited by their sexual misconduct. I do believe there is incredible damage when a man's morality does not line up with what he teaches.

But there's another way to look at this crisis: we are sitting on a tremendous opportunity. Can you imagine how many would believe in our Redeemer if *we* would truly drink of the Living Water, find redemption for our marriages, and then share our stories with others? If we come to intimately know Truth, then drop our jars and run through this culture shouting en masse, "Come see a man!"

I dream of that.

So does Bob.

We are both weary of the impotent, legalistic presence penetrating much of Christian culture. Our hearts long for honest, imperfect stories of God's redemption to radically release revival in our midst.

I think that's God's heart too. His Word says this:

> Let the redeemed of the LORD say so,
>   whom he has redeemed from trouble.
> —Psalm 107:2

Rise up, weary sister! Employ your tools of redemption. We have a call in the kingdom, and it's right in our own homes: to do the work of applying God's Truth to our lies so we can show the lost world that it's possible to live redeemed.

And oh, the living is so very sweet on the other side of redemption. In John 10:10, where we are warned of Satan's end goal with all these lies, we find our Redeemer making a bold declaration:

> "I have come that they may have
> life and have it abundantly."
> —Jesus

Abundantly!

To me that has meant I can live considerably beyond what I could have anticipated or expected. My happily even after is beyond my wildest imagination.

And this promise of abundance—our Redeemer's intention—is presented in contrast to the destruction the enemy brings. In other words, we can experience this kind of living in contrast to our formerly broken lives.

Do you believe this?

I do.

Because God has redeemed my understanding of His ongoing work in this world.

Redeeming What I Believe about Redemption

The story of Bob and Dannah's marriage is not over. The redemption work is *not* finished.

That really used to bother me. I wanted to be able to live one of those freedom stories that came with a sunset, white horse for two, and a sexy kiss just before "The End." But that is not the way it works.

Bob has been telling me this repeatedly as I write: "Don't sell them a bill of goods. Don't let them think that this is easy." And I've tried to comply.

We want it to be easy. We want redemption to rush into our lives. In fact, we often misconstrue Scripture to promise us the quick fix. Take for example this often-misused Bible verse:

> And we know that for those who love God all things work together for good, for those who are called according to his purpose.
> **—Romans 8:28**

We like to take that to mean God is working all our things out for us to experience something good. But that's not the promise.

The promise is that one day *all things* will work together. *All* things. Not *your* things. Or *my* things. Your things *and* my things *and* everybody's things will work together for *good*. But we will not necessarily be able to see the *good* until history has run its course. And then we will rejoice because we will understand that, in the long run, *all things* have moved this broken world in the direction of redemption!

Your story isn't over. The redemption work is not finished, and it won't be until the day of redemption.

But it will happen.

And it will be glorious!

Faith is to believe what you do not yet see;
the reward for this faith is to see what you believe.
—Saint Augustine of Hippo[13]

As you work through this part of the book you might want to listen to the *Happily Even After* limited-series podcast. Use this QR code to find and listen in to the one that corresponds to this chapter.

Growing in Truth:
Talk to Your Husband about **Truth and Freedom**

Living in the freedom that Truth brings is fairly simple *conceptually*. If there is an area of emotional unwellness or chronic sin, you *may* be believing a lie. If you've begun to embrace worldly mindsets that are in opposition to God's Word, you *are* believing a lie. Overcoming your bondage requires you to identify the lie and replace it with God's Truth. That's how you experience freedom.

But living in freedom that Truth brings is complex *practically*. Living it out is like warfare. And lies are by nature deceptive. You'll need to make this a lifelong battle. And you'll almost certainly need help.

What I've written about Truth and freedom in this book is the tip of the iceberg on identifying lies in our world and your belief system. I encourage you to pick up extra reading or listen to some podcasts to help you learn more.

In the meantime, talk through Truth #7 together with your husband:

The Truth will set you free.

1. Can you recall a time when you experienced a new sense of freedom in Christ because you identified a lie you were believing and began to understand the Truth according to God's Word?

2. Are there any lies you're battling now specifically related to the redemption journey you are on as a couple? I'll give you some help by sharing five common lies women and men believe about sexual sin.

   - "I can't tell anyone about this."
   - "My sexuality is separate from my spirituality. So this is no big deal."

- "This is just who I am. I cannot change."
- "God's standards for sex are out of date."
- "I have to have an outlet for my sexual desire."[14]

3. If you identified a lie above, find a Truth that resonates with your spirit. If you need some help, I've provided some thoughts below, but nothing works quite as well as searching the Scriptures and praying for God to reveal Truth to you. What matters most is that you begin to counter all deception by inserting God's Word into your thought process.

- God designed the church to help bring healing to those struggling with sin and shame (James 5:16).
- Your sexual past and current temptations do not define you. The cross does (1 Corinthians 6:9–12).
- Marriage and sex are a picture of the gospel (Ephesians 5:31–32).
- The most important thing about my sexuality is not how I feel, but what God says is true (1 John 3:20).
- My identity is as an image bearer of God (Genesis 1:26–27).
- God's standards were never "in style" (Genesis 19:5; 38:22; Leviticus 18; Judges 19:22; 1 Kings 11:1–8; 1 Corinthians 6:9).
- Sexual integrity is when my sexual choices are a consistent expression of my relational and spiritual commitments (Ephesians 5:3; 1 Thessalonians 4:3–5; 1 Corinthians 6:13–20).
- You can live without a sexual outlet, but you cannot live without the unfailing love of God (Proverbs 19:22).[15]

4. Pray together. Ask the Lord to reveal any lies you have been believing. If there are some lies you are believing, ask Him to reveal Truth and transform your mind (Romans 12:2).

recommended reading

- *Lies Women Believe and the Truth That Sets Them Free* by Nancy DeMoss Wolgemuth and/or *Lies Men Believe and the Truth That Sets Them Free* by Robert Wolgemuth. These books provide a three-step process to identify personal lies and replace them with Truth. I contributed a chapter on lies we believe about sex. The lies and truths in this conversation section are from that book.
- *Live No Lies* by John Mark Comer. This book will help you understand the lies of the culture and it will motivate you to live in Truth.

About Those Red Chairs

Inexplicable joy erupted from my spirit. Tears rolled down my cheeks.

Never in my wildest dreams could I have imagined God redeeming those red chairs. Not this thoroughly. Not this obviously.

After I had them brought back to the house, I began to sit in one each morning. Coffee in one hand, Bible in the other, I soaked in the presence of Jesus. Sometimes I even imagined Him sitting in the other chair next to me. In this way I was participating in their redemption.

Then our beautiful twin grandbabies had arrived, born prematurely. When they came home from the NICU, Addie and Zoe's four-pound bodies were nurtured in those very chairs. By their mom and dad. By aunts, uncles, grandmothers, grandfathers. By Bob. By me.

That had been such a sweet bonus.

And now it was even sweeter.

My daughter-in-love, Aleigha (the twins' mother), had just sent me something I'd asked her to write. It was a foreword for my book on parenting tween girls. She could not have imagined how healing these words would be to my heart:

Just a couple of years ago, Bob and Dannah opened their home to Robby and me when we brought our beautiful twin baby girls home from the hospital. Bob and Robby cared for our girls late into the night. Dannah woke up very early to help me with the first bottle feed of the day. We sat in two cozy red chairs, snuggled up close to her fireplace. For me, these chairs are Holy Ground, a precious place where I encountered the radical and undying love of Jesus. Dannah and I held my baby girls and talked and laughed and cried and prayed. She listened to my heart and spoke truth into it. Truth about my Savior who sustained the lives we held in precarious times, truth about my girls, truth about me.

When you pick up this book, dear reader, you are cozying up in Dannah's red chair in her living room. You are laughing and crying and receiving truth from her heart to yours, and the immense love of your own Savior, Jesus Christ.[1]

Oh, the immense Love of our Savior!

May you experience our Redeemer as beautifully and as thoroughly as I have, my friend. And then, may you tell someone your redemption story.

"I called on your name, O LORD,
from the depths of the pit;
you heard my plea, 'Do not close
your ear to my cry for help!'
You came near when I called on you;
you said, 'Do not fear!'
You have taken up my cause, O LORD;
you have redeemed my life."

—LAMENTATIONS 3:55–58

bonus content

Got Questions?

Even after reading this book, chances are you still have a lot
of questions. A few come up often enough in my discussions
that I felt compelled to provide this megaload of bonus
content to help you find answers.

"How do I know if I'm a Christian?"

God loves you so much, my friend.

Right here and in this moment, God's eye is on *you* (Psalm 17:8). He sees you and is filled with passionate and unconditional love. You have all of His love. Here on this earth, nothing and no one has the power to come between you and Him (Romans 8:31–39). He loves you without reference to your behavior (Romans 5:8). There's nothing you could ever do to make Him love you more or less.

I hope today you begin to fully understand and live in that love.

There is one thing that could eventually separate you from His love: death (2 Thessalonians 1:9). But God loves you *so much* that He's done something radical to avoid that. He's prepared a free gift for you.

I don't know about you, but I've never gotten a free gift without having to reach out to accept it. Let me tell you how to do that.

You've probably heard John 3:16 before, but indulge a girl and read it slowly. Linger on the words.

> For this is how God loved the world: He gave his one and only Son, so that everyone who believes in him will not perish but will have eternal life.
> —John 3:16

Jesus died for *you.*

Why?

He died because you sin. Each and every one of us does (Romans 3:23). Sin is behavior that goes against God's intended design and plan. It distances us from God and others. No matter what the sin is—lying or using porn, gossiping or having an affair, holding grudges or murder—it all has an equal impact. The potential for eternal separation from God.

But there's a way out. God made it possible.

Feeling the distance between God and you is an important step in His plan. You see, eventually you will get mired in and aware of your sin. You might feel empty, at the end of your rope, weak, hopeless, or . . . well, sinful. This is actually good news. God is helping you understand your need for Him. He wants you to feel the separation now so it doesn't become eternal.

This is precisely why sometimes the hardest experiences in our lives become the best. We often find our Redeemer, Jesus, when we hit rock bottom.

Keep that good news in mind while I tell you the bad news.

> For the wages of sin is death. . .
> —Romans 6:23

The Bible says that the punishment for your sin is death. The fact is, sinful behavior enslaves you to the service of Satan. But do you know how to set a slave free? You buy her freedom. Jesus paid for your life with His death.

Your Redeemer

To redeem something is to *buy it back*. Spiritually speaking, *redemption* refers supremely to the death of Christ on the cross, through which He purchased or ransomed us with the price of His own life.

The great news is that Jesus didn't stay dead. He came back to life with the power to forgive your sins. This frees us from the grip of spiritual bondage which results in death . . . if we want it to.

Which brings us to the second part of the Scripture I quoted above—the good news that can obliterate the bad:

> . . . but the free gift of God is eternal
> life in Christ Jesus our Lord.
> **—Romans 6:23**

Jesus offers this redemption to us as a free gift to save us from our own death. This does not mean that we won't *physically* die, but that that we will spend eternity with God in heaven. It also means that we can live our lives abundantly here on earth rather than live in bondage to our sin and suffering.

So how do you accept this gift?

You accept God's free gift of redemption by *believing* in Jesus and *receiving* Him as your Savior by verbally declaring your belief.

> If you confess with your mouth that Jesus is Lord
> and believe in your heart that God raised him from
> the dead, you will be saved.
> **—Romans 10:9**

Let me break down what it means to *believe* in Jesus:

- You understand that Jesus is God's Son.
- You accept that His death saves you from your sin.
- You give Jesus control of your life.

Do you believe in Jesus?

If so, you are ready to *receive* the free gift of Jesus as your Savior. You can start by praying something like this right now:

> Dear Lord, I admit to You that I am a sinner. I thank You for sending Jesus to die on the cross for my sins and for raising Him from the dead. I ask You to forgive me of my sins. I invite You to come into my life to be my Lord. Thank You for saving me. In Jesus' name. Amen.

If you prayed that, something supernatural just happened. You were redeemed.

Now tell someone! Reach out to someone you know who is a Christian and invite them to celebrate with you. You can also ask them for advice on what to do to grow in your faith.

recommended reading

- *Heaven and the Afterlife: The Truth about Tomorrow and What It Means for Today* by Erwin W. Lutzer

"Why do I need a counselor (and how can I find a good one)?"

If you don't already have a Christian counselor, I recommend that you find one.

You're not surprised, right? This was a major focus in Part One of this book. But I got kickback from early readers who were concerned about the cost. And it's true that counseling can be expensive.

But I beg you to consider: What's the cost of *not* getting help?

Let's just start with the financial cost of porn. Lots of guys start out using free porn, but many end up paying for it. Every second, $3,075.64 is spent on internet porn. Way back in 2006, it was estimated that revenues for sex-related entertainment businesses were just under $13 billion in the United States.[1] And that's just porn.

So you might want to ask your husband what kind of money, if any, he is spending on this addiction.

And I want you to consider a pattern that Bob and I have observed. Many men we know who control their own income—entrepreneurs, business owners, and salespeople—dramatically increase their income just from stopping their pornography use. Can you imagine what changing your family income could look like over the course of your life?

At least one psychologist who specializes in sex addiction therapy, Doug Weiss, agrees that pornography is a time-consuming, money-sucking addiction.[2] (Obviously, the same is true for those whose habits have escalated to strip clubs, escorts, and the like.)

And we haven't gotten to what porn and sex addiction is costing you and your husband in terms of your marital relationship, the impact on your family as a whole, or the spiritual life of your husband. And we hope it never goes there, but the cost of divorce can be financially and emotionally devastating for all involved!

With all this in mind, Bob and I have chosen to invest financially in our marriage by paying for the counseling we need. When necessary, we've asked for financial help from people who loved us. It's been our great joy to pass on that support to other couples we know when the opportunities arise.

All this is to reinforce that we hope you will consider finding a Christian counselor.

Start Looking for a Christian Counselor Today

This won't be an easy search, and it may take you weeks or months to find the right one. So get started right away.

We recommend that you look for a biblically based, clinically informed therapist. You want someone who puts the Word of God as the primary authority as they work with you, but who is clinically trained to understand the impact of addiction and betrayal trauma on the human body and mind.

Some experts recommend one of these designations for clinical training:

- **Certified Sex Addiction Therapists** (CSAT) are trained to work with your husband.
- **American Association for Sex Addiction Therapy** (AASAT) provides certification that helps therapists work with either addicts or partners or both of them together.
- Counselors certified by the **Association of Partners of Sex Addicts Trauma Specialists** (APSATS) have training specifically to work with you.

I can certainly see where this specialized clinical training could enhance your therapy work, but Bob and I did a great deal of our most successful work with therapists who did not have these designations. So consider it a bonus if you find a Christian therapist with training like this, but don't automatically reject those who don't. Just be sure they have clinical training and experience of some type.

The counselors Bob and I have worked with utilize many of the terms and tools of the recovery industry to move us forward in our freedom journey, and these have been helpful. But there's one tool that Jesus Himself says is essential to experience freedom: Truth.

Satan's primary weapon to keep you and your husband in bondage is deception. After all, wasn't it a lie in the Garden of Eden that led to the first sin?

Lies are powerful things. But God's Truth is more powerful than Satan's lies. It possesses the ability to separate us from the lies and bondage of this broken world. Through Jesus Christ and His Word, you and your husband can be set apart from sin and its effects. The big theological word for that is *sanctification.*

Jesus prayed this for His disciples—and for us—the night before He was crucified:

> "Sanctify them in the truth; your word is truth."
> **—John 17:17**

As you are sanctified by truth, you will experience freedom from the lies (John 8:31–32). That is the goal of finding redemption: full freedom! To experience that, I recommend a therapist who is unequivocally committed to the authority of the Bible.

Bob and I have not been successful at finding the right match in our hometown. There are a few good Christian therapists where we live, but either we didn't have the right chemistry or there were too many complex relationships at work for us to feel comfortable with our local options. But we did not let that stop us from finding the help we needed.

Don't let it stop you either!

In recent years, we've found, many therapists are willing to treat patients online. You have lots of options. Bob works online with Phil each week, and Phil lives in Nashville. I work with my beloved Tippy from time to time, and I'm planning an intensive for later this year. She lives in Missouri. The marriage counselor we have worked with, Pete, is in Colorado. We have made trips there as needed for in-person care.

To find a Christian counselor, you'll probably need to research and do a brief interview with several, then schedule sessions with a few. (If you get it right the first time, you are especially blessed!) You can begin by doing these two things:

1. **Research the therapist and do a brief phone interview before you schedule your first appointment.** Seek answers to your questions about their faith. You're not looking for someone who agrees with every detail of your theology, but I would look for someone who understands redemption in Jesus Christ and the authority of Scripture. These are the kinds of questions you can ask to get a feel for what a therapist believes and how they have been educated.

- Can you tell me about your relationship with Jesus Christ?
- What do you believe about the authority of the Bible?
- What role does prayer play in your counseling work?
- How do you think lies play into chronic behavioral problems?

You also need to ask a few questions to know about the therapist's clinical training, such as:

- Are you licensed to counsel patients in your state?
- What experience and training do you have to help individuals with sex addiction?
- What experience and training do you have to help individuals who are experiencing betrayal trauma?

2. **Consider your first several appointments as an extended interview.** You're not locked into working with a therapist if you don't sense they are committed to God's Word, if they don't have the right clinical training to meet your needs, or if you just aren't feeling the right chemistry. Counseling is an intimate and important relationship. Don't settle for anything less than a perfect fit. If you're not finding that, it's okay to keep searching.

Be persistent. It's worth it.

Consider Beginning with Intensive Therapy

The conventional model for therapy is a one-hour session each week. We found this to be a very slow way to make progress, especially when we were doing couples therapy. By the time our discussion got to something important, it seemed the session was over. Often we felt as if we were leaving surgery with our hearts still cut wide open.

Then, we discovered the *intensive therapy* model, which utilizes longer sessions for a limited time. For example, treatment might be concentrated into daily three-hour sessions five days in a row over a one- to four-week period. This is great if either of you needs urgent emotional care or if you just want to spend your vacation winning at marriage. After you complete an intensive, you can follow up effectively with the conventional model.

We found we were able to make more headway in two weeks of this kind of therapy than we did in a year of conventional sessions.

There are many counseling centers that offer intensives, and some therapists will cluster your care into an intensive if you make a request. We recommend this to kick off your work.

Here are a few of the places we have personally experienced intensives. We highly recommend each of these providers:

- **Crossroads Counseling of the Rockies**, Buena Vista, CO (crossroadscounselingoftherockies.com)
- **Faithful & True**, Eden Prairie, MN (faithfulandtrue.com)
- **Sage Hill Counseling**, Murfreesboro, TN (sagehill.co)

"Where can I find free or affordable support groups?"

Your husband needs his people.

And you need yours.

I've already told you that you need two types of people.

- You each need a group of men or women who have worked through or are working through what you are walking through.
- You also each need to include your closest, safest friends in what you are experiencing.

Finding Group Support

Many communities have great in-person support groups for wives whose husbands are using porn or involved in other forms of sexual sin. If your community does not, there are great online support groups available. I'll share a few I recommend below.

In full disclosure, I have not participated in either a local group (there aren't any) or online support (I prefer something more intimate).

Instead, I created my own network of women whose lives were similar to mine and who have walked through either a pornography addiction or other type of sexual sin with their husband. You may have to do this—to build your own program as I did.

But the vast majority of women find existing groups for partners work well for them.

Here are some great online options to consider if there is not a group in your hometown to join.

- **Fight for Love Ministries** (fightforloveministries.org). Check out their Facebook group for wives.
- **Live Free Wives** (livefreewives.org). Offers free and low-fee online groups for wives. This website also has one of the most comprehensive lists of ministries, support groups, and other resources for partners. Be sure to check it out.
- **Live Free** (livefreecommunity.org). Offers free and low-fee online groups, including an app for men struggling with sex addiction.
- **Pure Desire Ministries** (puredesire.org). Offers local and online groups for both your husband and you.

It is imperative that the groups you and your husband work with require 100 percent honest and humble disclosure. The truth cannot be watered down. Cheap grace cannot be tolerated. So many groups allow partial transparency or just pat someone on the back when they say something superficial like "I'm struggling" or "I had a bad week." That's not the kind of honesty that will produce victory. Thank them kindly and move on.

I'm sad to say that my husband found more success using a local twelve-step recovery group than in his Christian men's accountability groups. This is because he's found the men in the twelve-step groups have more humility and were broken enough that they were brutally honest about their struggle. Bob has utilized both a local twelve-step group and online twelve-step groups, and when we travel he sometimes finds a meeting where we happen to be.

But what about my hard line that counseling and group work be biblically based? That's precisely why Bob is *also* in a men's accountability group with our church. Each week he meets with godly men to pray, and that makes me feel so wonderfully safe. But I'm sympathetic to his need to be with men who are unafraid to be honest with their sin. And the men in his twelve-step recovery group definitely know he's a Christ follower. He makes no bones about who his "Higher Power" is, and he's not the only one. This is what has worked for my man.

You may also look at what I would call a hybrid of twelve steps and Christian accountability. There are many such programs available, including:

- **Celebrate Recovery**, a Christ-centered twelve-step recovery program. Learn more and find a group at celebraterecovery.com.
- **STEPS**, a biblically based approach to the twelve steps. Learn more at lifeway.com. (Search for "STEPS" on that website.)

Consider Beginning with a Retreat or Event

Sometimes a great way to find your people is to start with a retreat or an event. This can also hasten your educational curve as you learn about addiction and recovery and hopefully get filled up with the Word of God. If you cannot afford a counseling intensive, this is a great way to jump start your journey in a more cost-effective manner.

Here are some retreats and events we feel comfortable recommending.

- **Faithful & True**, Eden Prairie, MN (faithfulandtrue.com). Workshops available for men, wives, and couples.
- **Pure Desire Ministries**, various locations (puredesire.org). Find an upcoming event near you on the website.

Telling Your Friends

The Bible says that Satan walks about as a "roaring lion, seeking whom he may devour" (1 Peter 5:8). Lions typically hunt by singling out an animal that is isolated and alone. Sometimes they do this by stalking a group of animals and dispersing them. They're trying to isolate one victim.[1]

Don't let that be you. Tell someone you are struggling and why.

Not everyone, of course.

You will be blessed if you have two or three godly friends in your church whom you can talk to about real things. Pursuing this admittedly daunting task disarms Satan of one of his favorite weapons: loneliness.

Let me say it again, tell someone.

recommended reading

- *Fight for Love: How to Take Your Marriage Back from Porn* by Rosie Makinney. For finding support groups.
- *Connected: Curing the Pandemic of Everyone Feeling Alone Together* by Erin Davis. For encouragement to tell friends.

"Do I look like a fool?"

Many women who are married to men struggling with sexual sin say they feel like complete fools. Can you identify? *raises hand slowly*

Do you feel like a fool right now?

Compounding this pain is oversimplified advice from individuals or books that do not understand the complexity of the situation. Some say, "You just need to forgive him." Others, "You just need to leave him."

When people oversimplify your situation and the way you should be responding, it tends to cause toxic shame, which heightens that sense of feeling like a fool.

But the truth is, even without the opinions of others, you'd probably struggle with feeling foolish.

- foolish for not having a clue what was going on
- foolish for ignoring your sense that something wasn't right
- foolish for believing him when he promised to change
- maybe foolish for daring to believe your marriage really could be redeemed (which will be our main focus here)

For me, those foolish feelings were compounded by the fact I had built *an entire ministry* on the mission statement God had written on my heart back on the streets of Chicago. I'd written a bestselling book for teen girls on the topic of sexual integrity. My ministry team and I had trained groups of people the world over to help others live in what we called *pure freedom.*

I had to load up that pachyderm and bring it into the counseling room so Tippy could help me look at it with truthful eyes.

But let me tell you something I learned: feeling foolish can easily embed itself into your belief system. You may easily believe the lie that you *are* a fool, especially if you want to stay in your marriage.

Please let me introduce you to a woman whose story gave me the courage to confront that lie with something purposeful.

Meet Cindy Beall

One day I was scanning Amazon for lifelines when I came across a book titled *Healing Your Marriage When Trust Is Broken.* I wanted to read it right away, so I downloaded it to my iPad and began:

> If you are reading this book, chances are you are staring at an obstacle so big and so wide and so high that you don't think there's any hope. But, with God, there's always hope.[1]

I was immediately hooked.

This woman's story was very different from mine. Cindy's husband, Chris, was a worship leader who'd had an affair—and gotten the other woman pregnant. I hadn't experienced that! Still, I related to Cindy's words. They contained healing power for me.

I thought, *I want what this woman has!*

As I read on, I learned that Chris and Cindy's pastor, Craig Groeschel, hadn't quite known what to do when he learned about Chris's infidelity. But he reasoned that if people heard the truth in love, there would be nothing to gossip about. So he ever so carefully told *the whole church* what had happened.

This was not the forced public shaming some churches employ, but a call to the body of Christ to be a safe place for this hurting couple and to believe that God could make them "better than new." (That's redemption language, my friend.)

That church became a hospital not just for Chris and Cindy, but for anyone who was spiritually sick. (Oh, how we need more hospitals and fewer country clubs of faith!)

During this time Cindy was given some great advice from one of the church's leaders: *Don't make any big decisions about how to respond right now. Let your emotions stabilize.* (That sounds wise and clinically informed!) But Cindy needed some space. So she drove herself and her three-year-old son, Noah, to her parents' house. While she was there recovering, she visited her mom's pastor for counsel.

Pastor Dan's shepherding presence made it safe for Cindy to spew out her whole story. She wanted to know: *Should I stay or should I go?* His answer to her changed everything for me. This is what he said:

> What you've endured is very hard.
> But you are not a fool to stay and be a
> part of the redemptive work in a man's life.[2]
> **—Pastor Dan**

Tears flowed.

I never wanted to give up on my marriage. Not once. But I sure did struggle with feeling foolish. If you do, too, let this Truth sink into your heart and mind:

God has allowed this crisis in your life. That means that, for this season anyway, it is His call on your life to tend to and nurture your marriage.

If you're like me, that's not an easy thing to accept. I wanted to be off on a mission field doing something daring or holed up in a writing cabin writing a book or mentoring teens. But I resisted this assignment from God to participate in my husband's redemption story.

Why?

I felt like such a fool.

Reading Cindy's book, *Healing Your Marriage When Trust Is Broken,* transformed my mind. Her testimony changed my thinking to consider it an honor to participate in the redemption story of Bob Gresh.

You know, anytime God calls us to do something, it is a great honor. Soak in this thought:

> The call of Christ is always a promotion. Were Christ to call a king from his throne to preach the gospel to some tribe of aborigines, that king would be elevated above anything he had known before. Any movement toward Christ is ascent, and any direction away from Him is down.[3]
> —A. W. Tozer

"Why do I need help when this is his problem?"

Let me answer this question by telling you a story.

Melissa Ruff's husband had struggled with pornography since he was only seven or eight years old. His porn addiction was in the background through their years of dating and early marriage. Eventually he got the help he needed and experienced God's healing. Melissa says he "turned into a completely different person. He is now an amazing husband, an amazing father . . . all the things that every woman wants in a man!"[1]

But she didn't realize how damaging the cycle of pornography had been to her own heart and mind.

"I thought for sure because he had changed and he had healed and God had done this miraculous thing in his life, that I would have the same thing," says Melissa. "That I would be healed, and that I would just be okay. And we would have a great sex life. Turns out that's not what happened. . . . There was a lot of trauma that happened through all of the years of that cycle. And so I had to go and get my own counseling and my own help to start healing."[2]

Today Melissa is the director of Live Free Wives, an online community of women impacted by sexual betrayal and infidelity. She doesn't want other women to make the same mistake she did and delay the healing.

Own the Damage

Here's one of the most profound things our marriage counselor ever told me:

> If you want to experience healing,
> you have to own the damage.
> —Pete Kuiper

Frankly, that didn't seem fair when he said it to me. And I told him so. That dear man gave me the most wonderful word picture to fix my impaired thinking. Let me share it with you.

Imagine walking past a swinging door, the kind you see in restaurants that leads to the kitchen. As you pass, the door forcefully swings out and whacks you in the face. You bend over in excruciating pain and put your hand on your face. Something feels wet and slimy. You pull your hand away and see that it's covered in blood.

The waiter who opened the door is completely undone! "I'm so sorry," he exclaims over and over. He brings you clean cloths and ice for your nose. Again he apologizes profusely.

You accept his apology because, well, you're nice like that. But after a good half hour your nose is still gushing. It looks like you need to get it cauterized.

Who needs to go to the hospital? The waiter? Or you?[3]

You do, of course.

It's your face, and you have to own the damage because you own the nose.

It works the same way when someone wounds your mind and emotions. Your husband may be repentant. He may be deeply grieved by how his sin has hurt you. You may even be ready to forgive him. But your heart and mind *still* need special attention for you to experience healing.

Your healing work may include personal counseling, visiting your doctor, exercising, eating well, group therapy, and many other things. Once after a long conversation with a psychologist friend, I decided my personal care required buying a yellow blouse. Long story, but it made a difference!

The point is: you need to discover what you need and build *your* plan. But if you want to be healed, you first have to own the damage.

"Why does the sadness keep coming back?"

I think it is God's mercy that we don't feel all our sadness at once. But we still need to feel it. All of it. It generally comes in stages or waves.

You may not yet have recognized the grief in your heart because you're so numb and confused that you're not sure what to feel.

Or you may be too overwhelmed with fear and anger to understand what is happening.

Or you may still be thinking, as I did at first, that you have to hold it all together.

And that, my sister, is not only a lie but a barrier to your healing and to the redemption of your marriage.

Grief is a normal, human response to pain and loss. It's also an appropriate response to the brokenness and sin of our world.

Remember, Jesus wept at the tomb of His dear friend, Lazarus (John 11:35). The Savior of the world was sinless and perfect, and yet He grieved to the point of weeping.

Surely that should tell us something!

Grieving is a sinless, perfect response to the brokenness that confronts us in this fallen world.

I don't know about you, but I find it strange or even unnatural when I attend a funeral where people don't seem to be sad. But I'm deeply moved by men and women who authentically express the afflicting crush of their grief *while* they vocalize hope in Christ.

I saw that kind of authenticity when I watched the funeral of Dr. Lois Evans. Her celebration service was a mingling of tears and celebration. Her son, former NFL player and chaplain for the Dallas Cowboys, Jonathan Evans, delivered a eulogy that went viral.

> I'm letting you know that today I am afflicted, but I am not crushed. I am perplexed, but I will not be driven to despair because we have victory in Jesus Christ.[1]

Why did so many people want to hear this son's grief-filled lament? Because it was real. And it reminded us of something important: the world is not as it should be. Jonathan's honest grief invited us to pause from our endless busywork to remember we live in a sinful, fallen world. It also called out to us to consider how we should participate in God's redemptive work for humanity.

I need you to know this: godly women grieve.

Over death. Over loss.

But also over sin.

Wailing Women

In the Old Testament, God instructed His people not only to grieve, but to wail and lament during times of sin and injustice. The prophet

Jeremiah, who wrote about the nation of Israel dealing with all kinds of evil, wickedness, and deceit, also records:

> Thus says the LORD of hosts:
> "Consider, and call for the mourning women to come;
>   send for the skillful women to come;
> let them make haste and raise a wailing over us,
>   that our eyes may run down with tears
>   and our eyelids flow with water."
> —Jeremiah 9:17–18

The "mourning women" referenced in this verse were professional wailers, brought out to conjure up and express the emotions of the people. Apparently, the tears of the people of God were so dried up that they had to *pay* people to respond appropriately to what was happening in the world.

Don't let your own tears dry up over the state of your marriage! You need to be fully engaged in the sadness of this season—not just because your husband has grieved your heart, but because he has grieved God's. When you mourn, your heart is in alignment with His, and you are authentically calling upon Him to be your strength.

As Bob and I each tended to our own hearts, my own progress was delayed by believing the lie that I had to hold it all together emotionally. I thought that was what it meant to be "strong in the Lord."

During a counseling session with my dear Tippy, she confronted the lie I was living and invited me to try on something more truthful.

"Dannah," she challenged. "You need to learn to lament."

And then, she assigned me the task of studying the book of Lamentations. I did, and I'll tell you, that book is no party on the pages of the Bible! But it is a great training tool in authentic Christian living. Lamenting is how a Christ follower grieves the brokenness in our world.

Don't worry, I'm not going to ask you to study Lamentations! But I do want to help you recognize your own grief and get a sense of where you are in the grieving process. I also hope to give you some basic truth from God's Word so you know what to do to process your pain appropriately.

The Waves of Grief

It's fairly well known that grief comes in predictable stages.[2] But as anyone who has experienced deep pain and loss will tell you, those stages are almost never clearly defined. You don't just go through one, finish with it, and graduate to the next.

More commonly, the various experiences of grief hit you in waves that wash over you (sometimes bowling you over!) and then recede. It's not unusual to think you've finished with one, only to have it flood back in again. Only in time, as you work through your pain appropriately, do the waves of grief grow gentler and gradually subside.

Translation: it's going to get better.

I promise.

But first you've got to grieve.

"What stages of grief can I expect to experience?"

In question #6 we looked at your need to grieve and lament after the shock of discovering your husband's secret sin in marriage. We also recognized that grief is a process that typically comes in waves or stages. Let's look at that typical progression, keeping in mind that the process may not always be lockstep and linear. You may not progress in neat steps from one stage to another, and sometimes you may feel you're back in square one. But you will eventually make it through!

Wave #1 · Numbness/Denial

After the initial shock of discovering a husband has fallen prey to sin, many women go numb. Their emotions may freeze to the point that they not only don't feel pain; they don't feel much of anything.

This is not a new response, of course, nor is it unique to women. David wrote about it in Psalm 38:8. The Berean Study Bible translates the beginning of that verse as "I am numb."

Some women in these early stages may even find themselves in complete denial, embracing a different reality than the one they're living. As an act of survival, they pretend everything is okay!

So this stage of grief might include anything from convincing yourself it's all been a big mistake to jumping into problem-solving and even premature forgiveness. You may be doing all the "right things" and still barely know what's hitting you. The overall sense is:

"It's all going to be okay."

But it's not okay, is it?

The most helpful thing you can do at this stage is allow yourself time to let reality soak in and let your feelings catch up with you. (They will!) Listen to the counsel of trusted friends who can help you see what you cannot. Remind yourself that numbness and even denial are normal responses to a painful shock. And resist the urge to just rush in and fix the situation before you have felt it. But don't stay in this stage. Admit the hurt and get the help you need to move on.

The rest of Psalm 38:8 reads, "I groan in anguish of heart" (BSB). David didn't give in to the numbness when he was crushed. He allowed his spirit to awaken . . . and groan in anguish.

You, too, must give yourself permission to grieve.

Wave #2 · Self-Blame

Once the shock wears off, grief is known to hand out magnifying glasses and invite women to look closely at the past. And for some, this becomes an invitation to blame themselves for what has happened.

This can be as simple as thinking: *I obviously saw this coming! How could I not do something to stop it?*

If you're at this point, you might feel like a schmuck! The overall sense you might experience during this phase is:

"It's my fault!"

Many women experience lengthy seasons of self-blame. And this self-inflicted torment is an unhealthy and unhelpful distraction from the real issues in the marriage.

Here's where some would attempt to comfort you with, "It's not your fault." And that is true up to a point. Your husband will have to stand alone before God to explain what he's done to offend your marriage vows (Romans 14:12). His sin *is* his fault.

But coming to terms with God's Truth is often so much more complex than applying the Band-Aids of quick comfort. That's why I won't tell you, "It's not your fault."

The goal, you see, is not to blame anyone except the ultimate source of your grief and point your finger of accusation in *that* direction. First Peter 5:8 reads, "Be sober-minded; be watchful. Your adversary the devil prowls around like a roaring lion seeking someone to devour."

Satan has devoured your husband's heart and mind for a time. He has prowled around and set his eyes on your marriage. He is ultimately to blame for this pain you find yourself in.

Your husband will need to take *responsibility* for what he's done if he has not already. He needs to confess and own his sin. So do you—for any sin of your own that God is legitimately convicting you of. But overwhelming, guilt-inducing *blame* for either of you doesn't fit into God's redemption grid. Romans 8:1 declares, "There is therefore now no condemnation for those who are in Christ Jesus."

Wave #3 · Anger

From the silent treatment to explosive bursts of anger, the wave of anger comes in all shapes and sizes but rarely goes without notice. It is certainly not difficult to identify this wave.

The overall sense a woman feels during this wave of grief is:

"You selfish jerk!"

(And that's the PG version!)

Anger as an emotion is natural and even useful. It's the "fight" part of the "fight or flight" response to danger or pain—a surge of energy meant to keep us safe. *Feeling* angry is nothing to be ashamed of or denied. Neither is honestly expressing your angry feelings by "using your words."

But out-of-control anger is a completely different thing, especially when it takes the form of yelling, name calling, the silent treatment, throwing objects, or laying hands on another person. Such expressions of anger are unproductive at best and can be incredibly destructive.

Unfortunately, I know something about this. You see, Bob and I were once advised by a man who thought it would be helpful for me to call Bob a derogatory cuss word. He spent most of our first (and only) session together urging me on until I finally looked at Bob and unenthusiastically repeated the word this misguided man had been trying to get me to say.

It was like opening a floodgate! By week's end I was *shouting* that word at Bob . . . and not without enthusiasm! Unfortunately, I was also growling it under my breath at drivers to express road rage, *something I've never actually had a problem with!*

Here's the problem with the uncontrolled expression of anger. It *keeps* you angry! In fact, it makes you angrier. And anger is usually just a secondary emotion—evidence that you've been wounded and need to give yourself permission to grieve.

Ephesians 4:26 reads, "Be angry and do not sin." You have God's permission to be angry. And you also have a warning to be careful while you're processing it.

Your husband sinned. The Bible communicates over and over that God gets mad at sin. You can be angry about it too. But remember, you're not God. And the way you communicate and express your anger is prone to sinfulness. What sense does it make to respond to sin with sin?

This is a unique life opportunity for you to learn to express your anger in the right way and at the right time. Write your frustration out in a journal. Beat a pillow. Talk it out with a friend. Take up boxing. But process your anger appropriately. Otherwise, you'll still be stirring up the one who started all this in the first place: the devil.

Here's a good verse to put on your index cards if you find yourself stuck in the anger stage.

> Be angry and do not sin; do not let the sun go down on your anger, and give no opportunity to the devil.
> —Ephesians 4:26–27

Let the anger remind you who the true enemy is in this chapter of your story. And while you're at it, let it lead you to understand your pain a little better.

In most cases, women find that anger is a buoy at the top of their ocean of emotions, but deep down in the depths is something they really don't want to face: fear. So if you're experiencing anger, you might want to ask yourself this question: *What am I afraid of?*

Maybe you are afraid your husband will walk away from his Christian faith. Or perhaps your fear is about what people would think of *your* Christian faith if you fell apart instead of holding it together.

(Anger makes magnificent emotional superglue.) You may be terrified that your husband will leave you, that you will need to leave him, or that you'll just never recover.

Such fears are not always rational (although they can be). But when we begin to be honest about what we're feeling and verbalize it (to a counselor, a support group, and eventually our husbands), the anger-beast inside won't have anything to feed it.

My own biggest fear was that our relationship would never be the same again. And in a way, that one was a reasonable fear. After what we were going through, how could it help but be different? But then I realized my fear and anger were distracting me from the wonderful truth that God could actually redeem our relationship.

That I wasn't fighting for the marriage I used to have but for something new and better.

And that what I was afraid of wasn't likely to happen but, if it did, God's grace would carry me through even that!

That's when I finally got to where my grief was telling me to go....

Wave #4 · Deep Sadness

When we finally arrive at the place of deep sadness—and for me it was fairly quickly—we'll often find the pain to be insufferable and relentless. The nights will be darker here. And lonelier. The waves will loom higher. You will have a lot of questions that threaten to overwhelm you.

And this is where you learn to lament.

Lament · "a cry of sorrow and grief."[1]

That's the dictionary definition anyway. But for the Christian lament goes beyond the sorrow and grief. Christian lament is mingled with faith. It's not just a helpless crying out, but also a hopeful looking up to the Lord. It's actually a form of prayer!

You can use Bible verses on your index cards to cry out prayers of lament. (I hope you are still collecting verses to memorize and meditate upon!) The Psalms are an especially rich source—in fact, a Google search for "psalms of lament" will reveal a treasure trove of verses. To turn them into prayers, all you need to do is read them aloud or paraphrase them.

For instance, you could base your lament on Psalm 102:4, 12: "Lord, my heart is withered like grass in the heat, and I cannot remember to eat my food. But I believe You are still sitting on Your throne and that You are ruling forever."

As you learn the pattern from Scripture, you can then go on to build your own prayers of lament. "God, today I'm experiencing deep waves of fear and frustration, the likes of which I've never known. Please calm the storm in my heart like You calmed the storm on the sea for the disciples."

And this, friend—this is where Jesus walks on water! In the waves.

I urge you to be like Peter in the boat filled with fear, his eyes peeled to see our God in flesh there in the dark (Matthew 14:22–23). Hear Jesus say to you, "Don't be afraid." Tell your fear and your sadness to submit to the Savior.

And then He will invite you to walk on top of those deep, dark waves as only He can. He'll say, "Come!" And I hope you go to Him.

Now, you'll still have a lot of questions that seem impossible to answer. That's when you'll find yourself sinking and wonder why you didn't stay in the boat.

It is the foolish woman who does not welcome the questions and wrestle with them. But this is not the time to look for answers. Do you think Peter was doing anything but clinging to Jesus in those high waves of fear? I urge you to store your questions for a later time. For now, hold on to Him as Peter did.

As I learned to do when I felt myself sinking.

Jesus came to Peter in the waves. He came to me in mine. He is "near to the brokenhearted" (Psalm 34:18). There, in my mourning, I could feel Him in the stillness. In the dark.

Especially when I lamented.

If you still don't believe me that God issues permission slips to grieve, look up Ecclesiastes 3:1–4. Read about how there is a time for everything.

> For everything there is a season,
> and a time for every matter under heaven:
>
> a time to be born, and a time to die;
> a time to plant, and a time to pluck up what is planted;
> a time to kill, and a time to heal;
> a time to break down, and a time to build up;
> a time to weep, and a time to laugh;
> a time to mourn, and a time to dance.
> **—Ecclesiastes 3:1–4**

Right now, it's probably your time to grieve over sin and brokenness.

"Should I be practicing self-care (and how)?"

For some reason this question makes me think of the lame man whose story is told in John 5:1–16. He continuously waited at the Pool of Bethesda with "a multitude" of sick and needy people. Each day they waited for the water to be stirred up, believing that the first one into the pool would experience miraculous healing.

Now, there is no record in the Bible that anyone was actually healed in this way, but this man had chosen his method of recovery. It just wasn't working for him. He'd been an invalid for thirty-eight years!

Then Jesus showed up and asked the man a question: "Do you want to be healed?" (verse 6). What a funny thing to ask of someone who is lying by a healing pool!

The lame man didn't really answer the question. He just explained all the reasons why his chosen method of healing hadn't worked. Yet.

Jesus knew that deep down this man desperately wanted to be healed. He told him, "Get up, take up your bed, and walk" (verse 8). And according to John, "At once the man was healed, and he took up his bed and walked" (verse 9).

There's nothing wrong with taking care of ourselves, practicing healthy rhythms of rest and care. In fact, God *wants* us to do that.

And it's important to realize that you really are in a season of needing recuperation for your body and soul.

I encourage you to pursue healing experiences like long walks to clear your mind, massages to experience comforting touch, or even a weekend at the beach with girlfriends to come up for air. I gifted my own broken heart with those exact activities during my intense season of neediness.

But take care not to sit too long beside a pool of self-care. Sometimes you've got to get up, take your bed, and walk.

And how do you know when to do what? For that matter, how do you find the strength to do what you need to do?

You do need some special care right now. And it's your responsibility to own that reality and find ways to take care of yourself. But don't let that reality cause you to turn inward and try to do it all on your own strength. (There's no sufficiency to be found within you.)

Instead I invite you to access the omnipotent Spirit of the living God!

Redeeming Our Understanding of Self-Care

Let's redeem our understanding of self-care with some precious words from Jesus. He spoke them to His disciples the last night He was with them. They had no idea of the kind of suffering and persecution that lay ahead. But Jesus did, and here's what He told them:

> "I tell you the truth: it is to your advantage that I go away, for if I do not go away, the Helper will not come to you. But if I go, I will send him to you."
> **—John 16:7**

Wait a minute!

It was to their *advantage* that the Savior of the world would leave them? Really?

Yes, really. Because after Jesus went away, He sent the Helper—the Holy Spirit—in His place.

Here's the deal: God chose when you would be born with intention and purpose (Jeremiah 1:5; Psalm 139:15–16). I don't pretend to know what your purpose is, but I do know that God plopped you—and me—onto the planet during the ever-so-short-in-the-scheme-of-things time when it is to our "advantage" that Jesus is not here in the flesh.

So we'd better figure out what that means!

I pulled together some Scripture to help us. Take a look. It really seems that the Spirit's help could make all the difference when our bodies and souls need some extra care *and* when we need support and guidance to take up our beds and walk. Here are just a few ways the Spirit is able to help as we seek redemption and healing in our marriages:

- He comes alongside us to advocate for us (John 15:26 NIV).
- He intercedes for us when we run out of words to pray for ourselves (Romans 8:26).
- He opens our minds to understand the Scriptures, something we may need a lot of help with when our brains are hijacked (Luke 24:45; John 14:26).
- He helps us experience freedom from anything that holds us in bondage, including fear, codependency, or hypervigilance (2 Corinthians 3:17).
- He leads us into Truth, helping us bypass all the confusing lies (John 16:13).
- He works to make us more like Jesus in everything we do rather than reacting to our husbands out of our emotions and fears (Romans 8:14–16).
- He sweetly convicts us—and our husbands—of sin so we can confess and find freedom (John 16:8).
- He helps us and our husbands (and others in the body of Christ) experience unity of heart and mind (Acts 4:31–32).

If it was to our advantage that Jesus left so the Spirit could come, it's certainly to our advantage that we get ourselves out of the seat of power for the work of healing we need. You must let God's Spirit direct you when to sit down and rest. And when to rise up and walk.

Rest for Your Soul

You don't just need rest for your body, which I must remind you is one of the Ten Commandments: "Remember the Sabbath day, to keep it holy" (Exodus 20:8). You also need *rest for your soul*. And you cannot experience that without the presence of God.

Read these words from your Redeemer:

> "Come to me, all who labor and are heavy laden, and I will give you rest. Take my yoke upon you, and learn from me, for I am gentle and lowly in heart, and you will find rest for your souls. For my yoke is easy, and my burden is light."
> —Matthew 11:28–30

Notice the invitation to "come" is mingled with both the promise of rest *and* the language of work. A yoke is a funny thing to mention when someone's looking for rest, don't you think?

You won't find ultimate rest for your soul from walks in the woods or bubble baths, even though those can be useful activities. True rest for your soul comes from being tied to the all-knowing, always loving God of the universe. Period. His rest is supernatural and comes when and where you need it if you are obeying His promptings.

This matters so much because you probably have limitations on how much you can practice self-care anyway. Children. Finances. A job. Any number of responsibilities. The Holy Spirit can still lead you to experience rest anyway.

To see what I mean, open your Bible to Mark 6:30–44 and read about how exhausted the disciples were. They told Jesus about what they've been doing in His name. They must have mentioned (or grumbled about) being so busy they didn't have time to eat! (Does that sound like your life sometimes?)

In response, Jesus extended the invitation: "Come away by yourselves to a desolate place and rest for a while" (verse 31).

Whew! I bet they were relieved. They followed Jesus out into the wilderness. But their "retreat" didn't work out the way they'd probably imagined. That's because people saw them going to their place of rest and recognized them.

> Not one or two or ten people, but five thousand.
> And that was just the men.
> Their wives and kids were there too!

Before the disciples knew it, Jesus was preparing to feed that crowd—with five loaves of bread and two fish and a handful of weary followers. That was obviously not enough food, and the disciples were at the end of their limited supply of energy.

And yet the Bible says "they *all* ate and were *satisfied*" (verse 42).

Satisfied! Even at the end of themselves, the disciples were satisfied. Having a front row seat to see God's miraculous work tends to satisfy a person.

God has done that for me over and over—filled me with satisfaction when I was at the end of me.

He'll do it for you, too, as you find rest in the One whose burden is always light.

thank you

This is the book I once desperately wanted to read, but never wanted to write. Were it not for the encouragement of many dear friends and co-laborers, it would not exist. I literally wrote it afraid and am especially thankful for the courage I borrowed from:

My friends at Moody Publishers. Paul Santhouse, you not only encouraged this book but you gave my sweet husband courage when we walked through this fire of refinement. You are a true brother in Christ. And Judy Dunagan, my dear sister in Jesus, you were patient with me over and over when fear set in! Special thanks to Randall Payleitner, Erik Peterson, Connor Sterchi, and Ashley Torres for all the work you've done to bring this book to be.

Dr. Juli Slattery. Thank you for advising me on subjects related to psychology and for putting Christ in the driver's seat of how you interpret behavioral science. You not only helped me steward this message with care; you also walked beside me through the difficult days I write about in this book. You are a true friend.

Dr. Chris Miller. Your theological review—on a tight deadline—gave me confidence as I put my heart on paper. Thank you not only for your commitment to handling the Word of God accurately, but also for loving it.

The review team. Eileen King, Janet Mylin, Erin Davis, Dawn Wilson, Phil Krause, Laura Booz, and Aubrey Brush—your precious time was greatly appreciated as you made this message better, wiser, and more useful.

Anne Christian Buchanan. You have an editor's mind but the heart of a creator. What a blessing you have been in the final days of perfecting.

My Pure Freedom Ministry Team. You have tolerated my mental absence so well! And you have also sacrificed extra hours and brainpower to enable me to write this book. Special thanks to Wade Harris and Shani McKenzie, who have kept the ministry rolling without me.

Praying friends (you know who you are). You lifted me and this message up to Jesus while I was writing. Thank you so much!

Tippy Duncan, Pete Kuiper, Mike Bivens, Phil Herndon. You are giants! Thank you for counseling our hearts and writing these pages into our lives with us. Were you not with us in the trenches, the lessons in this book would not be in our hearts and minds.

Bob. You are so courageous. To let me write this for the sake of the kingdom and hearts that need healing is something few men would do. And you didn't just allow it. You labored beside me . . . and went without meals. I love you. We are happily even after.

Jesus. I still cannot stop weeping tears of joy as I sit here in my red chair and imagine You there in Yours. No one writes better endings than You, my Redeemer. I love You with all my heart!

notes

chapter one

Epigraph: D. Martyn Lloyd-Jones, *Spiritual Depression: Its Causes and Cure* (Grand Rapids, MI: Eerdmans, 1965), 143.

1. This concept was introduced to me by our beloved marriage counselor, Pete Kuiper, from Crossroads Counseling Center in Buena Vista, Colorado. He first taught us this wonderful truth during our first intensive therapy course there. Many years later, we brought Pete to our hometown to train our ministry team and staff at some local churches. Many of my quotes from Pete in this book, including this one, are from the yellow notepad I filled during those later lectures. They are used with his permission. For more wisdom from Pete, I highly recommend his book, *At the Crossroads: Finding Your Way Home to Who You Really Are* (Friendswood, TX: Baxter Press, 2018).

2. You may be wondering why I would suggest that "maybe" you will enjoy your marriage again. That's because it takes two people to pursue a healthy relationship. But it's so important to keep in mind that this freedom is available to you whether or not the outcome for your marriage is what you desire.

chapter two

1. John Gottman and Nan Silver, *The Seven Principles for Making a Marriage Work: A Practical Guide from the Country's Foremost Relationship Expert* (New York: Harmony Books, 2015), 13.

2. Gottman and Silver, *Seven Principles for Making a Marriage Work*, 13.

3. A. W. Tozer, *Paths to Power* (Chicago: Moody Publishers, 1940), 19–20.

4. Mark R. McMinn, *Why Sin Matters: The Surprising Relationship Between Our Sin and God's Grace* (Wheaton, IL: Tyndale, 2004), 110–11.

5. Covenant Eyes, *Porn Stats: 250+ Facts, Quotes, and Statistics about Pornography Use* (2018 Edition), eBook (Owasso, MI: Covenant Eyes, 2022), 13, downloaded from www.covenanteyes.com/pornstats.

6. Covenant Eyes, *Porn Stats*, 22.

chapter three

Epigraph: Rosie Makinney, *Fight for Love: How to Take Your Marriage Back from Porn* (Nashville: B&H, 2020), 3.

1. Barbara Steffens and Marsha Means, *Your Sexually Addicted Spouse: How Partners Can Cope and Heal* (Far Hills, NJ: New Horizon, 2009), 62. (Note: Though we feel these authors' research is valid and useful, we find that many of their solutions and teachings are not biblical or balanced.)

2. Ashley Jameson, "Women's Takeover #1: Healing from Betrayal with Dr. Barbara Steffens," *Pure Desire Podcast*, YouTube, February 1, 2022, 4:47–5:00, www.youtube.com/watch?v=2Qg27oapLVA.

3. Hilal Dogan, "This Is Your Brain on Trauma," DVM360, October 2, 2019, www.dvm360.com/view/your-brain-trauma.

4. Bradley D. Grinage, "Diagnosis and Management of Post-Traumatic Stress Disorder," *American Family Physician*, December 15, 2003, www.aafp.org/pubs/afp/issues/2003/1215/p2401.html#sec-6; and Megan Hull, ed., "PTSD Facts and Statistics," Recovery Village, May 26, 2022, www.therecoveryvillage.com/mental-health/ptsd/ptsd-statistics.

5. Katherine Blakeman, "Your Brain on Porn," National Center on Sexual Exploitation, December 19, 2017, https://endsexualexploitation.org/articles/your-brain-on-porn.

6. Kendra Cherry, "What is Neuroplasticity?," Verywell Mind, February 18, 2022, www.verywellmind.com/what-is-brain-plasticity-2794886.

7. Ferris Jabr, "Cache Cab: Taxi Drivers' Brains Grow to Navigate London's Streets," *Scientific American*, December 8, 2011, www.scientificamerican.com/article/london-taxi-memory.

8. Gary Wilson, "The Great Porn Experiment," talk delivered at TEDxGlasgow, March 4, 2012, YouTube, 16:28, www.youtube.com/watch?v=wSF82AwSDiU.

9. Rachel Anne Barr, "Watching Pornography Rewires the Brain to a More Juvenile State," The Conversation, November 27, 2019, https://theconversation.com/watching-pornography-rewires-the-brain-to-a-more-juvenile-state-127306.

10. Makayla Simpson, "What You Should Know about Women and Pornography," Ethics and Religious Liberties Commission, September 20, 2018, https://erlc.com/resource-library/articles/what-you-should-know-about-women-and-pornography.

11. Elizabeth Martin and Robert Hine, *A Dictionary of Biology*, 6th ed. (Oxford, UK: Oxford University Press, 2008), s.v. "supernormal stimulus," Oxford Reference (online), 2014, https://www.oxfordreference.com/view/10.1093/acref/9780199204625.001.0001/acref-9780199204625-e-4294.

12. Oxford Reference Overview, s.v. "supernormal stimulus," accessed August 8, 2022, https://www.oxfordreference.com/view/10.1093/oi/authority.20110803100543339.

13. Judith Reisman, "'Gay' Gypsy Moths and Porn Addiction," The Reisman Institute, April 17, 2013, www.drjudithreisman.com/archives/2013/04/gay_gypsy_moths.html.

14. Tom W. Coleman et al., *Gypsy Moth*, Forest Instinct and Disease Leaflet 162, US Department of Agriculture, Forest Service, April 2020, www.fs.fed.us/nrs/pubs/jrnl/2020/nrs_2020_coleman-t_001.pdf.

15. Reisman, "'Gay' Gypsy Moths and Porn Addiction."

16. Ted Shimer, "Porn is Rewiring a Whole Generation, Christians Included," *Relevant*, May 19, 2022, https://relevantmagazine.com/life5/porn-is-rewiring-a-whole-generation-christians-included.

17. Covenant Eyes, *Porn Stats: 250+ Facts, Quotes, and Statistics about Pornography Use* (2018 Edition), eBook (Owasso, MI: Covenant Eyes, 2022), 4, downloaded from www.covenanteyes.com/pornstats.

18. Jay Stringer, *Unwanted: How Brokenness Reveals Our Way to Healing* (Colorado Springs: NavPress, 2018), 6.

chapter four

Epigraph: Karen Ellis, "A Powerful Weapon," Kingdom Praying with Karen Ellis, transcript of podcast episode, Revive Our Hearts, October 2, 2022, www.reviveourhearts.com/podcast/revive-our-hearts/powerful-weapon.

1. Alice Park, "What Divorce Does to Women's Heart Health," *Time*, April 14, 2015, https://time.com/3821251/divorce-heart-attack.

2. Amanda MacMillan, "What Is Inflammation? 13 Ways Inflammation Can Affect Your Health," Health, March 4, 2015, www.health.com/mind-body/13-ways-inflammation-can-affect-your-health.

3. Sotirios Tsalamandris et al., "The Role of Inflammation in Diabetes: Current Concepts and Future Perspectives," *European Cardiology*, 14, no. 1 (2019): 50–59, https://doi.org/10.15420/ecr.2018.33.1.

4. Nitin Singh et al., "Inflammation and Cancer," *Annals of African Medicine*, 18, no. 3 (2019): 121–26, https://doi.org/10.4103/aam.aam_56_18.

5. The term "betrayal trauma" was first introduced by psychologist Jennifer Freyd in 1991. For a short summary of this experience from a purely secular viewpoint, see Crystal Raypole, "How Betrayal Can Cause Trauma and How to Start Healing," Healthline, updated October 21, 2021, www.healthline.com/health/mental-health/betrayal-trauma.

6. Ethan Kross et al., "Social Rejection Shares Somatosensory Representations with Physical Pain," *Proceedings of the National Academy of Sciences (PNAS)* 108, no. 15 (March 28, 2011): 6270–75, https://doi.org/10.1073/pnas.1102693108.

7. Karen Ellis, "A Powerful Weapon."

chapter five

Epigraph: Nancy DeMoss Wolgemuth and Robert Wolgemuth, *You Can Trust God To Write Your Story: Embracing the Mysteries of Providence* (Chicago: Moody Publishers, 2019), 185.

1. Not an exact quote, but an often-cited paraphrase from Athanasius of Alexandria, quoted in Joel C. Elowsky, ed., *Letter to Marcellinus on the Psalms: Spiritual Wisdom for Today* (New Haven, CT: ICCS, 2017) 285–86.

chapter six

Epigraph: Erin Davis, *Connected: Curing the Pandemic of Everyone Feeling Alone Together* (Nashville: B&H, 2014), 154–55.

1. *Lexico*, s.v. "shame," accessed July 10, 2022, www.lexico.com/en/definition/shame.

2. Brené Brown, "Shame Resilience Theory: A Grounded Theory Study on Women and Shame," *Families in Society—The Journal of Contemporary Social Services* 87, no. 1: 43–52, quoted in Joaquin Selva, "Shame Resilience Theory: How to Respond to Feelings of Shame," Positive Psychology, June 14, 2017, https://positivepsychology .com/shame-resilience-theory.

3. American Psychological Association, s.v. "trauma," *APA Dictionary of Psychology*, accessed July 10, 2022, https://dictionary.apa.org/trauma.

4. "What Is Trauma?," pdf info sheet, Therapist Aid, accessed July 10, 2022, www .therapistaid.com/worksheets/what-is-trauma.pdf.

5. Juli Slattery, "#398. How Trauma-Informed Care Helps Your Brain, Body and Relationships," interview with Victoria Gutbrod, *Java with Juli* (podcast), Authentic Intimacy, January 31, 2022, www.authenticintimacy.com/resources/39821/398-how-trauma-informed-care-helps-your-brain-body-relationships?source=blog.

6. Victoria Gutbrod, in Slattery, "#398. How Trauma-Informed Care Helps Your Brain, Body and Relationships."

7. Xiaoli Wu et al., "The Prevalence of Moderate-to-High Posttraumatic Growth: A Systematic Review and Meta-analysis," *Journal of Affective Disorders*, 243 (January 15, 2019): 408–15, Science Direct, https://doi.org/10.1016/j.jad.2018.09.023.

8. Rosie Makinney, *Fight for Love: How to Take Your Marriage Back from Porn* (Nashville: B&H, 2020), 7.

9. Makinney, *Fight for Love*, 93.

chapter seven

Epigraph: Joni Eareckson Tada, *Making Sense of Suffering* (Torrance, CA: Rose Publishing, 2012), "Scriptures on God's Purpose in Our Pain: Suffering and My Faith," location 147 of 305, Kindle.

1. C. S. Lewis, *A Grief Observed* (New York: Bantam, 1976), 9.

2. Pete Kuiper, CrossRoads Counseling Class, August 2017. Used with permission.

chapter eight

Epigraph: John Newton, "Letter Twenty-Eight: Ryland's Marriage—Advice on the Married State," in Grant Gordon, ed., *Wise Counsel: John Newton's Letters to John Ryland, Jr.* (Edinburgh: Banner of Truth Trust, 2009), 138–39.

1. Kay Arthur, *Our Covenant God: Living in the Security of His Unfailing Love* (Colorado Springs: WaterBrook, 2003), 3.

2. "A Smoking Fire Pot," Ligonier, August 11, 2006, www.ligonier.org/learn/ devotionals/smoking-fire-pot.

3. Kathy Keller, "Marriage in Gospel Focus," pre-conference speech delivered at The Gospel Coalition National Women's Conference 2012, Orlando, Florida, June 22,

2012, YouTube, 31:13/41:35, www.youtube.com/watch?v=G8hmo0Ji-uo.
4. Kathy Keller, 31:20/41:35.
5. Timothy Keller, "Love and Lust," sermon delivered May 6, 2012 at Redeemer Presbyterian Church, YouTube, 4:40/34:40, www.youtube.com/watch?v=jUWnE 6GeOiE.
6. Timothy Keller, "A Covenant Relationship" sermon delivered September 9, 2007 at Redeemer Presbyterian Church, YouTube, 6:21/30:55, https://www.youtube .com/watch?v=xICD5Ycsu04.

chapter nine

Epigraph: Pete Kuiper, CrossRoads Counseling Class, August 2017. Used with permission.
1. Ibid.
2. Peter H. Kuiper, *At the Crossroads: Finding Your Way Home to Who You Really Are* (Friendswood, TX: Baxter Press, 2018), 25–26.
3. Nancy DeMoss Wolgemuth, *Lies Women Believe: And the Truth That Sets Them Free*, updated and expanded ed. (Chicago: Moody Publishers, 2018), 233.
4. *Lexico*, s.v. "bitterness," accessed July 10, 2022, www.lexico.com/en/definition/ bitterness.
5. Jacinta Jimenez, "Compassion vs. Empathy: Understanding the Difference," Better Up (blog), July 16, 2021, www.betterup.com/blog/compassion-vs-empathy#:~: text=Compassion%20definition%3A%20compassion%20is%20an,creates%20 a%20desire%20to%20help.
6. Douglas Weiss, *Intimacy Anorexia: Healing the Hidden Addiction in Your Marriage* (Anaheim, CA: Discovery Press, 2010), chapter 1 callout, Kindle.
7. Weiss, *Intimacy Anorexia*, chapter 3.
8. Jay Stringer, *Unwanted: How Sexual Brokenness Reveals Our Way to Healing* (Colorado Springs: NavPress, 2018), 25.
9. Revealing Reality, *Young People, Pornography, and Age-Verification*, pdf report prepared for the British Board of Film Classification (January 2020), 15, www .revealingreality.co.uk/wp-content/uploads/2020/01/BBFC-Young-people-and-pornography-Final-report-2401.pdf.
10. Susan Knight, "5 Stages of Pornography Addiction," *Imperial Valley Press*, April 6, 2015, www.ivpressonline.com/life/stages-of-pornography-addiction/article_ cab7748c-2515-50b0-b8c4-fad6f988aef5.html.
11. Robert Weiss, "Sexual Addiction: Tolerance and Escalation," *Counselor: The Magazine for Addiction and Behavioral Health Professionals*, September 15, 2015, https:// www.counselormagazine.com/en/sexual-addiction-tolerance-and-escalation.
12. Jimmy and Kelly Needham, "When Your Spouse is Addicted to Pornography," For Better or for Worse with Jimmy and Kelly Needham, transcript of podcast episode, Revive Our Hearts, November 4, 2020, www.reviveourhearts.com/ podcast/revive-our-hearts/when-your-spouse-addicted-pornography.
13. Jimmy Needham, "The Real Battle for Sexual Purity," Jimmy Needham (blog), June 7, 2016, www.jimmyneedham.com/articles/the-real-battle-for-sexual-purity.

14. Needham and Needham, "When Your Spouse is Addicted to Pornography."

chapter ten

Epigraph: A. W. Tozer, *Man: The Dwelling Place of God* (Louisville, KY: GLH, 2019), 15.

1. Rosie Makinney, *Fight for Love: How to Take Your Marriage Back from Porn* (Nashville: B&H, 2020), 65.
2. Debra Laaser, *Shattered Vows: Hope and Healing for Women Who Have Been Sexually Betrayed* (Grand Rapids, MI: Zondervan, 2008), 207.
3. Laaser, *Shattered Vows*, 207.
4. This list is paraphrased from Susan Knight, "5 Stages of Pornography Addiction," *Imperial Valley Press*, April 6, 2015, www.ivpressonline.com/life/stages-of-pornography-addiction/article_cab7748c-2515-50b0-b8c4-fad6f988aef5.html.

chapter eleven

1. Will Krieger, "Lessons from the Playground," Repass, April 28, 2016, http://repassinc.com/2016/04/4125.
2. Robin Weidner, "Setting Godly Boundaries in Marriage," Focus on the Family, January 1, 2008, www.focusonthefamily.com/marriage/setting-godly-boundaries-in-marriage.
3. Gaslighting is a term taken from an old movie called *Gaslight* (1944). It basically means to make someone question her own perceptions, reality, or even her sanity.
4. "How Pornography Impacts Violence against Women and Child Sex Abuse," Focus for Health Foundation, accessed July 30, 2022, www.focusforhealth.org/how-pornography-impacts-violence-against-women-and-child-sex-abuse.
5. Mark Laaser, *Healing the Wounds of Sexual Addiction* (Grand Rapids, MI: Zondervan, 2004), 172.
6. I have adapted this definition from *APA Dictionary of Psychology*, s.v. "detachment," APA, accessed July 10, 2022, https://dictionary.apa.org/detachment.
7. *Lexico*, "meek," accessed July 10, 2022, www.lexico.com/en/definition/meek.
8. Strong's Exhaustive Concordance, s.v. praus (Strong's #G4239), Bible Hub, accessed June 10, 2022, https://biblehub.com/greek/4239.htm.
9. Daryl DelHousaye, "Continuing Insight: Loving Like Jesus in Our Marriage," in *Marriage: Its Foundation, Theology, and Mission in a Changing World*, ed. Curt Hamner et al. (Chicago: Moody Publishers, 2018), 61.
10. DelHousaye, "Continuing Insight," 62.

chapter twelve

Epigraph: C. S. Lewis, *Mere Christianity* (New York: HarperOne, 2015), 115.

1. John Murphy, "7 Health Dangers Aggravated by Stress," MDLinx, June 11, 2020, www.mdlinx.com/article/7-health-dangers-aggravated-by-stress/5MRhVjD6ZY9cNTGjucJDT5.
2. Murphy, "7 Health Dangers."

3. Robert H. Shmerling, "Autoimmune Disease and Stress: Is There a Link?," Harvard Health Blog, October 27, 2020, www.health.harvard.edu/blog/autoimmune-disease-and-stress-is-there-a-link-2018071114230.

4. Chadi G. Abdallah and Paul Geha, "Chronic Pain and Chronic Stress: Two Sides of the Same Coin?" *Chronic Stress* (2017), 1, htttps://doi.org/10.1177/2470547017704763.

5. "Forgiveness: Your Health Depends On It," John Hopkins Medicine, accessed July 29, 2022, www.hopkinsmedicine.org/health/wellness-and-prevention/forgiveness-your-health-depends-on-it.

6. Joe S. McIlhaney Jr. and Freda McKissic Bush, *Hooked: The Brain Science on How Casual Sex Affects Human Development* (Chicago: Northfield Publishing, 2019), 35.

chapter thirteen

Epigraph: Paul David Tripp, *Sex in a Broken World: How Christ Redeems What Sin Distorts* (Wheaton, IL: Crossway, 2018), 20.

1. Merriam-Webster, s.v. "trust (n.)," accessed July 10, 2022, www.merriam-webster.com/dictionary/trust.

2. Gary Wilson, *Your Brain on Porn: Internet Pornography and the Emerging Science of Addiction* (Margate, UK: Commonwealth, 2015), chapter 1, "What Are We Dealing With?," location 1099 of 4427, Kindle.

3. Wilson, *Your Brain on Porn*, "What Are We Dealing With?," location 1150 of 4427.

4. John Gottman, "John Gottman on Trust and Betrayal," *Greater Good Magazine*, October 29, 2011, https://greatergood.berkeley.edu/article/item/john_gottman_on_trust_and_betrayal.

5. John Gottman, "John Gottman on Trust and Betrayal."

6. David Guzik, "Proverbs 3—Wisdom from Trusting God," in *The Enduring Word Bible Commentary*, 2020, https://enduringword.com/bible-commentary/proverbs-3/.

7. Dennis Jaffe, "The Essential Importance of Trust: How to Build It or Restore It," *Forbes*, December 5, 2018, www.forbes.com/sites/dennisjaffe/2018/12/05/the-essential-importance-of-trust-how-to-build-it-or-restore-it/?sh=3dcd0a4064fe.

8. C. S. Lewis, *The Four Loves*, reissue ed. (New York: HarperOne, 2017), 155–56.

9. Ellie Lisitsa, "'Sliding Door' Moments," The Gottman Institute, accessed July 29, 2022, www.gottman.com/blog/what-makes-love-last-sliding-door-moments.

10. Lisitsa, "'Sliding Door' Moments."

11. A trigger is a stimulus—like a scene in a movie or seeing the chair where confession occurred—that causes your emotions to react in a very real manner to what happened in the past. Being triggered can make you feel like you're back at square one, but you're not! Don't let triggers lie to you. Read the message of the emotion. Is there more work to be done in that area? Do it.

chapter fourteen

Epigraph: Timothy Keller, "Love and Lust," sermon delivered May 6, 2012 at Redeemer Presbyterian Church, YouTube, 8:42–44/34:40, www.youtube.com/watch?v=jUWnE6GeOiE.

1. Larry Pierce, *The Outline of Biblical Usage*, s.v. *yada* (Strong's H3045), Blue Letter Bible, accessed July 10, 2022, www.blueletterbible.org/lexicon/h3045/kjv/wlc/0-1.

2. Juli Slattery, *Rethinking Sexuality: God's Design and Why It Matters* (Colorado Springs: Multnomah, 2018), 105.

3. Keller, "Love and Lust," 10:42–47/34:40.

4. Keller, "Love and Lust," 9:23–9:52/34:40.

5. Chris Taylor and Jenifer Taylor, "Jesus Passes through Samaria," The Bible Journey, accessed August 17, 2022, www.thebiblejourney.org/biblejourney1/4-jesuss-journeys-around-galilee33795/jesus-passes-through-samaria.

6. Bruce Marshall, *The World, the Flesh, and Father Smith* (Boston: Houghton Mifflin, 1945), 108.

7. Juli talks about these two core commitments in a book she wrote. You might like to read it: Juli Slattery, *25 Questions You're Afraid to Ask About Love, Sex, and Intimacy* (Chicago: Moody, 2015), 118–22.

8. *Thayer's Greek Lexicon*, s.v. *akatharsia* (Strong's Greek #4508), Bible Hub, accessed July 31, 2022, https://biblehub/greek/167.htm.

9. Greek Word Studies, "Defilement (3436) Molusmos," Bible Portal, accessed July 31, 2022, https://bibleportal.com/sermon/greek%2Bword%2Bstudies/defilement-3436-molusmos.

10. Strong's Concordance and HELPS Word-studies, s.v. *rhuparos* (Strong's Greek #4508), https://biblehub/greek/167.htm.

chapter fifteen

1. Skip Moen, "Just Do It," Hebrew Word Study, September 29, 2014, https://skipmoen.com/2014/09/just-do-it.

2. John Mark Comer, *Live No Lies: Recognize and Resist the Three Enemies That Sabotage Your Peace* (Colorado Springs: WaterBrook, 2021), 114.

3. Matt Jenson, *The Gravity of Sin: Augustine, Luther, and Barth on "homo incurvatus in se"* (New York: T&T Clark, 2007), 2.

4. David P. Goldman, "The Prophet of Ordinary Unhappiness," *Claremont Review of Books* (spring 2018), https://claremontreviewofbooks.com/the-prophet-of-ordinary-unhappiness.

5. Judith A. Reisman and Mary McAlister, "Deconstructing Dignity by Eradicating Shame: The Pernicious Heritage of Alfred Kinsey," *Faculty Publications and Presentations* 4:6, https://digitalcommons.liberty.edu/cgi/viewcontent.cgi?article=1003&context=psych_fac_pubs.

6. Jeremy Wiles, "What The Media Won't Tell You About The Sexual Revolution" The Conquer Series, July 31, 2018, https://conquerseries.com/what-the-media-wont-tell-you-about-the-sexual-revolution.

7. Reisman and McAlister, "Deconstructing Dignity," 9.

8. Reisman and McAlister, "Deconstructing Dignity," 8.

9. Comer, *Live No Lies*, 29.

10. Susan Brinkman, "Sordid Science: The Sex Research of Alfred C. Kinsey," *Alfred C. Kinsey and American Sex Ed*, The Reisman Institute, posted August 14, 2005, http://www.drjudithreisman.com/archives/2005/08/sordid_science.html.

11. Stephen Galloway, "Hugh Hefner: The Sad Secrets of his Final Years Revealed," *The Hollywood Reporter*, October 5, 2017, https://www.hollywoodreporter.com/movies/movie-news/hugh-hefner-sad-secrets-his-final-years-revealed-1046373.

12. Austin Fruits, "The Porn Epidemic: Problem, Consequence, and Hope," Josh McDowell, November 13, 2019, www.josh.org/the-porn-epidemic-problem-consequence-and-hope.

13. Saint Augustine, *Essential Sermons, The Works of Saint Augustine: A Translation for the 21st Century*, trans. Edmund Hill (Hyde Park, NY: New City Press, 2007), 164.

14. Nancy DeMoss Wolgemuth, *Lies Women Believe: And the Truth That Sets Them Free*, updated and expanded ed. (Chicago: Moody Publishers, 2018), 156–58.

15. Nancy DeMoss Wolgemuth, *Lies Women Believe*, 156–58 (adapted).

epilogue

1. Aleigha Gresh, forward to Dannah Gresh, *Six Ways To Keep The "Little" In Your Girl* (Eugene, OR: Harvest House, 2010), 9.

question #2

1. Covenant Eyes, *Porn Stats: 250+ Facts, Quotes, and Statistics about Pornography Use (2018 Edition)*, eBook (Owasso, MI: Covenant Eyes, 2022), 4–5, downloaded from https://www.covenanteyes.com/pornstats.

2. Doug Weiss, "How Much is Porn Costing You? The Costs of Pornography on Your Life," YouTube, 12:18, .youtube.com/watch?v=n30ZdMxWbDc.

question #3

1. Angela M. Cowan, "Carnivore Lions," National Geographic Resource Library, updated May 20, 2022, https://education.nationalgeographic.org/resource/carnivore-lions.

question #4

1. Cindy Beall, *Healing Your Marriage When Trust is Broken: Finding Forgiveness and Restoration* (Eugene, OR: Harvest House, 2021), 11.

2. Beall, *Healing Your Marriage*, 43.

3. A. W. Tozer, *Man: The Dwelling Place of God* (Louisville, KY: GLH, 2019), 10.

question #5

1. Melissa Ruff, "Unmissable Ministries #6 Live Free Wives," Fight for Love (podcast), episode 44, October 27, 2020, 8:24–34/39:51, https://fightforloveministries.org/podcast. I have edited this quote a little to make it more concise.

2. Ruff, "Unmissable Ministries #6," 8:40/39.51, edited.
3. Pete has given me his permission to share this illustration with you. It is also found in his book, *At the Crossroads: Finding Your Way Home to Who You Really Are* (Friendswood, TX: Baxter Press, 2018), 25–26.

question #6

1. Jonathan Evans, "Dr. Lois Irene Evans: A Celebration of Life and Legacy," funeral elegy delivered January 6, 2020, YouTube, 3:30:52, www.youtube.com/watch?v=FGxsa8vLU4Y.
2. The psychiatrist Elisabeth Kübler Ross is famous for introducing the theory of grief stages in her 1969 book, *On Death and Dying*. While I have learned from her insights and used some of her terminology, my concept of the waves of grief differs from hers. It is based on my personal experience and research as well as the wisdom of several Christian men and women who have counseled me.

question #7

1. *Vocabulary.com*, s.v. "lament," accessed July 10, 2022, www.vocabulary.com/dictionary/lament.

Get to the root of your anger, sadness, or other complicated feelings, and discover true biblical healing.

START NOW

SIX STEPS
TO OVERCOMING
Negative
emotions

DANNAH GRESH

www.dannahgresh.com/podcasts

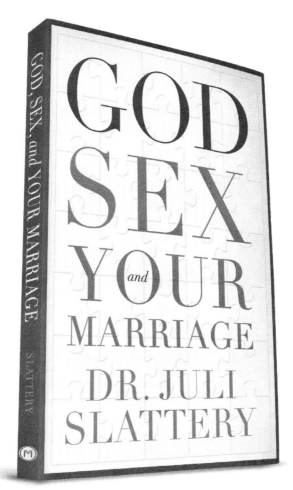